Myth and Reality in Wound Care

Myth and Reality in Wound Care

by

Clare Williams and Trudie Young
Cartoons by
Alan Palmer

Quay Books

Quay Books
Division of Mark Allen Publishing Limited
Jesses Farm, Snow Hill, Dinton, Nr Salisbury, Wilts SP3 5HN

© Mark Allen Publishing Ltd, 1998

British Library Cataloguing-in-Publication Data
A catalogue record for this book is available from the British Library

ISBN 1-85642-083-3

Printed in the UK by Redwood Books, Trowbridge, Wiltshire

CONTENTS

FOREWORD

As with many other aspects of nursing, wound care is surrounded by myth and ritualistic practice. This book is a small step in the fight to ensure that all nursing practice is undertaken from sound research-based evidence.

It can be very difficult and frustrating when the research is available but still health care professionals refuse to change. This is an area that needs careful consideration by the change agent.[1]

In our years of experience in the field of wound care we have come across many myths and rituals that form the basis of practice. Some or all may be familiar to you.

The aim of this book is to give readers the research-based evidence, where it exists, to enable them to challenge and question their colleagues and, eventually, successfully change practice.

It is a serious book, but we hope it makes you laugh at times. Most of all, we hope it empowers you with the knowledge you require to make the change in wound care.

Clare Williams and Trudie Young

1. Williams C (1994) Putting theory into practice: the management of change in a hospital ward. *J Wound Care* **3(7):** 344–5

SELF-ASSESSMENT QUESTIONNAIRE

The aim of this questionnaire is for you to identify deficits in your knowledge of wound care.

After reading the book you will, hopefully, have expanded your knowledge; by repeating the questionnaire you can evaluate whether learning has taken place.

Question one

List the four stages of wound healing

1

2

3

4

Question two

List five factors that delay wound healing

1

2

3

4

5

Question three

List two benefits of wound exudate

1

2

Question four

List three characteristics of an ideal wound environ- ment

1

2

3

Question five

List two local and two systemic signs of wound infection

local

1

2

systemic

1

2

Question six

List three methods of wound cleansing

1

2

3

Question seven

How do you treat a wound infection?

Topical antibiotics ❑

Systemic antibiotics ❑

A combination of the two ❑

Question eight

List three mechanical causes of pressure sores

1

2

3

Question nine

List three pressure sore risk assessment scales

1

2

3

Question ten

How long does it take for a pressure sore to develop

1 hour	❏
2 hours	❏
6 hours	❏
12 hours	❏
24 hours	❏
48 hours	❏
1 week	❏

Question eleven

List six types of leg ulcers

1

2

3

4

5

6

Question twelve

Below which of the following ABPI readings is it unsafe to apply compression bandaging?

1.5   ❏

1.0   ❏

0.8   ❏

0.5   ❏

Question thirteen

List three compression bandaging regimens

1

2

3

Question fourteen

How often should a dressing be changed?

every day   ❏

every two days   ❏

every five days   ❏

every week   ❏

other   [＿＿＿＿]

INTRODUCTION

The aim of this book is to provide research-based information, where it exists, to guide the practitioner through the uncertainties that enshroud wound care.

The book is divided into five chapters, covering many aspects of tissue viability

Chapter one looks at the wound-healing process, a sound knowledge of which is the key to wound management.

Chapter two considers the myths and realities surrounding the controversial area of wound cleansing and wound infection, a constant area of debate.

Chapter three looks at the aetiology, prevention and management of pressure sores.

Chapter four reviews the difficult area of leg ulcer diagnosis and management.

The final chapter is dedicated to wound dressings. This is an expanding area as companies battle to find the ideal dressing.

Each chapter takes 20 commonly held beliefs about wound care, and examines them in turn to determine whether they are fact or fiction.

At the end of the book you will find a self-assessment questionnaire. The aim of this quiz is to test your knowledge before and after reading the book. It is hoped that you will see for yourself that learning has taken place.

This book is suitable for all health care professionals who deal with the prevention and management of wounds in both the hospital and the community setting.

CHAPTER ONE
WOUND HEALING

1
Within the four stages of wound healing, each stage does not commence until the previous stage has been completed

Separation of the wound-healing process into four stages distinct stages is false. It is done to aid understanding of the wound- healing process. It is a method of simplifying a very complex process. In reality the process is a cascade of events with one stage merging into the next. The four stages are the inflammatory phase, destructive phase, proliferative phase and maturation phase. In some texts the second and third or third and fourth phases are amalgamated.[1]

The inflammatory phase of the process is a protective mechanism. Its aim is to minimise the injury and initiate a healing response. During the second phase the white blood cells that were summoned to the injured tissue during the inflammatory phase begin to clean up any devitalised tissue at the wound bed. By the third phase the wound is ready to commence rebuilding: a collagen and elastic mesh is formed and held together by ground substance. New blood vessels grow into the mesh to complete the formation of granulation tissue. In the final phase the granulation tissue is covered by pink epithelial tissue which migrates in from the periphery of the wound, pulling together the edges.[2]

The phases are interdependent: the triggers that activate one phase will stimulate or slow down another phase of the healing process. The key cells in the process, ie. platelets, macrophages and fibroblasts, all have multiple functions and between them orchestrate the wound-healing process.

To date it is the complexity of the wound-healing process that has thwarted scientists in their attempts to identify the single most important factor in the process.

Wound healing

Platelet
activation
  Neutrophils arrive
    Macrophages arrive
      Epithelial cells proliferate
        Fibroblasts arrive
        Collagen and ground substance
        are produced
          New blood vessels develop
                        Collagen matures
                            Scar
                            matures

0 1   2   15   21   365

DAYS

1.   Cooper DM (1990) Optimising wound healing. A practice within nursing's domain. *Nurs Clin N Am* **25**(1): 165–80
2.   Goode AW (1990) The metabolic basis of wound healing. In: Bader DL, ed. *Pressure Sores Clinical Practice and Scientific Approach*. Macmillan Press, London: 165–76

2
Healing is complete when epithelial tissue covers the wound

The pale-pink epithelial tissue migrates across granulating tissue as part of the final phase of wound healing, the maturation phase. Once covered by epithelial tissue, the wound appears healed to the naked eye. Underneath the epithelial tissue, however, the healing process is continuing, and wound remodelling is taking place. The scar is maturing.[1]

Initially, in wound repair, the first type of collagen that is laid down to form the bulk of the granulation tissue is type three. This is seen as an emergency measure and the collagen is laid down in a haphazard fashion. During remodelling, enzymes called collagenases break down type three collagen and replace it by a stronger, more robust form, type one collagen. There is a delicate balance between collagen degradation and regeneration. If the balance is upset, wound breakdown occurs. In normal tissue the collagen fibres lie in organised parallel strips which provide the wound with its strength. The realignment of collagen in wound repair strengthens the weakest part of the wound. The wound will only ever achieve 80% of the strength of uninjured tissue. The realignment causes further contraction of the wound, which can enhance distortion of the skin.

Healing is not complete once epithelialisation has covered the granulation tissue. The wound bed is still highly active and requires continued protection while it matures; maturation can take many months to achieve.

1.   Silver I (1994) The physiology of wound healing. *J Wound Care* **3**(2): 106–9

3
All wounds will heal if provided with the right environment

Too often the dictum is: provide the wound bed with a warm moist environment, and healing will automatically occur. Unfortunately this is not always the case. Providing the wound bed with the ideal environment without addressing the underlying cause of the wound will result in a perpetuating wound. Identification of the underlying problems requires a comprehensive patient assessment.[1] This will highlight the presence of chronic disease processes, such as cardiac failure, chronic obstructive airway disease, venous hypertension, diabetes mellitus and rheumatoid arthritis.[2]

If the disease process is not remedied the wound will not heal. Sometimes the disease process may be irreversible. For patients with such diseases, eg. fungating carcinoma of the breast, wound healing will never be a viable option, while amputation may be the only answer for advanced arterial impairment that presents with gangrenous tissue. The cause of the wound will provide vital information. For example, if the wound is a pressure sore caused by the patient's inability to alter position following a cerebro-vascular accident, healing will be delayed, until the pressure is relieved. The physiological response to psychological stress can delay wound healing.[3]

Essential to the process of wound healing is involvement of the patient and/or carer. Their needs and priorities should be identified, joint goals set and personal involvement maximised to reduce the stress and feelings of helplessness of the wounded patient.

The aim of wound management for the majority of patients is a pain-free wound-healing process resulting in an acceptable cosmetic outcome. For some patients this will never be achieved. The nurse must use her knowledge to provide the patient with the optimum environment for healing. Patient education has a key role to play in empowering the patient during his/her wound experience.

1. Shakespeare P (1994) The slow healing wound. *Practice Nurse* 8(2): 85–93
2. Krasner D (1995) Minimising factors that impair wound healing: a nursing approach. *Ostomy Wound Manage* 41(1): 22–30
3. Kiecoit-Glaser JK, Marucha OT, Molarkey WB *et al* (1995) Slowing of wound healing by psychological stress. *Lancet* 346(4): 1194–6

4
A wound has to reduce in size to show any improvement

The final outcome of a wound is skin closure and resumption of bodily function of the injured area. This can take many months to achieve. Healing during the life span of the wound takes the form of various guises. As the wound improves, reduction in size is only one way to measure improvement in the wound.

The first phase of wound healing is the inflammatory phase. The wound edges will appear red and inflamed, and the wound will produce copious amounts of exudate. Resolution of the external indicators of inflammation will indicate that the wound has progressed to the next stage of wound healing, ie. an improvement.

The wound bed may be covered with slough and necrotic tissue. These are viewed by the body as foreign to the wound, and the inflammatory phase will continue until they are removed. A percentage reduction, on a regular basis, of the slough and necrotic tissue indicates a cleansing of the wound bed and therefore improvement. Removal of the slough and necrotic tissue will enlarge the surface area and depth of the wound. This could be misinterpreted as an increase in the size of the wound bed, equating to a backward step in the healing process. However, the opposite is true. Patients should be warned about the initial increase in the size of their wound, to avoid causing them unnecessary anxiety.[1]

The proliferative phase of wound b
production of granulation tissue. The f
commenced is the presence of tiny r
base which increase in number until
bed is red and beefy in appearance,
ment.

The maturation phase of wound healing is signified by the migration of epithelial cells from the edge of the wound. In this instance a pale-pink rim is the indication of improvement in the wound-healing process. In venous leg ulcers, which are often shallow wounds, islands of pink epithelial tissue may grow in the centre of the wound from the base of hair follicle shafts.

Infected wounds can be malodorous and produce copious amounts of wound exudate. Once the causative bacteria has been identified from a wound swab, oral antibiotics can be prescribed. Signs of improvement at the wound bed would then be a reduction in odour and exudate production.

Eventually, wounds that follow the normal healing process will reduce in size. Along the way there are other factors which indicate that healing is taking place and the wound is improving. A knowledgeable nurse will be aware of these indicators, and ensure that an accurate report of the wound status is given to the patient and the multidisciplinary team. Education is therefore of primary importance in wound care.[2]

1. Millward P (1995) Common problems associated with necrotic and sloughy wounds. *Br J Nurs* **4**(15): 896–900
2. Williams C, Young T (1993) The development of a tissue viability module. *Proceedings of the 3rd European Conference on Advances in Wound Management.* 19–22 October, Harrogate. Macmillan Magazines, London: 146–7

5
Wounds heal quickest when left to dry out

This is a myth and research has proven that wounds heal quicker when provided with a moist wound environment.

The concept of moist wound healing was introduced by Winter.[1] He conducted his research in pigs, making surgical incisions in their skin. The incisions removed the epidermis and part of the dermis. The pigs had multiple wounds; some were covered with a polythene film and some were left exposed to the air. Winter then measured how quickly the wounds became covered with new epithelial tissue. Biopsies were taken and these indicated that epithelialisation occurred twice as quickly in the wounds covered with the film dressing.

This information was revolutionary in wound care. It was repeated by Hinman and Maibach who obtained similar results in human subjects.[2]

Winter had established the link between moisture and increased rate of epithelialisation in wounds. Further research looked at the effects of moisture on other aspects of the wound-healing process and in different types of wounds.

A study of burn injuries in animals found that the depth of necrosis was greater and the rate of healing slower in burns that were left exposed to the air and allowed to dehydrate. However, there was no evidence of necrosis in burns after one week when they were prevented from drying out by the application of a graft to keep the wound bed moist.[3]

Alvarez *et al*[4] looked at deeper examined the dermis in pigs. They c occlusive dressings *vs* wet-to-dry repair. They found that collagen syr occlusive dressings, confirming that a moist environment speeds up the formation of new granulation tissue.

Madden *et al*[5] compared the effects of occlusive and semi-occlusive dressings *vs* gauze dressings on partial-thickness donor sites. The found that under occlusion there was an increase in wound-healing rates and a decrease in patients' pain.

An American study by Gates and Holloway[6] reinforced the findings of Madden *et al*. Their patients had open abdominal wounds following caesarean section/hyster-ectomy surgery. The wounds were treated with a hydrogel or cavity filler and covered with a film dressing or a saline-soaked gauze (wet-to-dry dressing). The hydrogel/cavity filler and film dressing regimens were reported to be less painful and more cost-effective than the wet-to-dry regimen.

With leg ulcers, occlusive dressings are thought to facilitate degradation of the fibrin that forms part of the cuff which induces tissue breakdown and venous leg ulceration.[7]

Many wound care products provide an occlusive environment, and these should be used extensively to facilitate speedy wound healing.

1. Winter GD (1962) Formation of the scab and the rate of epithelialisation of superficial wounds in the skin of the young domestic pig. *Nature* **193**: 293–4
2. Hinman CD, Maibach H (1963) Effect of air exposure and occlusion on experimental human skin wounds. *Nature* **200**: 377–8
3. Zawacki BE (1974) Reversal of capillary stasis and prevention of necrosis in burns. *Ann Surg* **180**: 98–102
4. Alvarez OM, Mertz PM, Eaglstein WH (1983) The effect of occlusive dressings on collagen synthesis and re-epithelialisation in superficial wounds. *J Surg Res* **35**: 142–8
5. Madden MR *et al* (1989) Comparison of an occlusive and a semi occlusive dressing and the effect of the wound exudate upon keratinocyte proliferation. *J Trauma* **29**(7): 924–1
6. Gates JL, Holloway GA (1992) A comparison of wound environments. *Ostomy Wound Manage* **38**(8): 34–7
7. Hermans MHE (1993) Air exposure versus occlusion: merits and disadvantages of different dressings. *J Wound Care* **2**(6): 362–5

6
Acute wounds are active and chronic wounds are static

Acute wounds, eg. surgical wounds, are externally induced and heal in an orderly fashion, whereas chronic wounds are the result of an underlying disease process and are present for an extended period of time and do not always heal. Examples of chronic wounds are fungating wounds, pressure sores and leg ulcers.

In acute wounds the inflammatory reaction to wounding is normal, and necessary for initiation of healing. It is therefore a beneficial inflammatory response.

Chronic wounds are not static. They are actually hyperactive wounds. The inflammatory process that initiates the healing process is constantly being stimulated by the underlying problem, eg. low oxygen levels in pressure-induced ischaemia. This constant stimulation produces a continuous response, a prolonged and excessive inflammatory phase of wound healing that does not progress to the subsequent stages of healing.

Chronic wounds are therefore highly active, although their activity does not follow the normal pattern of healing.

7
Haematological investigations are an important part of the wound assessment process

Too often, wound assessment focuses solely on the wound bed and its surrounding skin. As a result the nurse treats only what is visually apparent, aiming only for symptom control and not wound healing.

If the assessment process is to have a positive outcome the patient should be viewed holistically, with wound inspection the final part of the process. Wound management has increasingly become part of the nursing domain, but this should not lead to nurses adopting an isolationist attitude. A multidisciplinary approach is required to ensure that the holistic assessment is met with a holistic response, involving the multitude of professionals within the health care team.

A part of the assessment process that requires medical input is the facilitation of haematological investigations. The investigations that are linked to wound assessment are as follows:

Investigation	Rationale	Implications
Full blood count	Identify anaemia	Reduced oxygen delivery to tissues
White blood cell count	Identify immunocompromised patients	Autolysis and wound infection
Serum albumin	Identify protein/calorie malnutrition	Impaired collagen formation
Serum ferritin	As above	As above
Serum reactive protein	Establish patients' immune status	Active rheumatoid arthritis

Investigation	Rationale	Implications
Arterial blood gases	Identify low tissue oxygen levels	Reduced oxygen delivery to tissues

A collaborative approach to patient care is required to ensure that underlying disease processes that have an adverse effect upon wound healing are identified and, where possible, corrected.

8
Age-related changes in the skin of an elderly person are sufficiently significant to delay wound healing

Many studies have attempted to document age-related changes in the skin. Various conclusions have been drawn, but they are often contradictory. An extensive review of the literature by Ashcroft *et al*[1] concludes that while it is frequently stated that ageing impairs wound healing, this assertion is usually unsubstantiated. Their main criticisms of the work they reviewed are that animal models are often used and there is no general agreement as to which changes are age-related.

There is loose agreement that the skin of an older person is characterised by the following changes. The epidermis and dermis are thinner, with a weaker connection between the two structures. This may allow the two layers to separate more easily following shearing/friction damage.[2] There is also a decrease in the immune function of the skin.[3]

Although these changes are acknowledged, what is not proven is their effect on wound healing. The changes themselves may not cause a problem, but they may be important when coupled with the multiple disease processes that can accompany ageing.

To categorically state that wounds heal more slowly in an older person than a younger person would be inaccurate and give a false representation of the current state of knowledge of wound healing in older people.

1. Ashcroft GS, Horan MA, Ferguson MWJ (1995) The effects of ageing on cutaneous wound healing in mammals. *J Anat* **187**: 1–26
2. Jones PL, Millman A (1990) Wound healing and the aged patient. *Nurs Clin North Am* **25**(1): 263–77
3. Bennett G, Moody M (1995) *Wound Care for Health Professionals*. Chapman & Hall, London

9
A bleeding wound is a healthy wound

The presence of bleeding at a wound bed indicates that an arterial blood supply is present. This blood supply is important for preservation of the tissue. It is the mechanism by which the wound is supplied with vital nutrients and oxygen.

Evidence of the effectiveness of the blood supply is the rate of regeneration of new granulation tissue, ie. the speed of the wound-healing process. Under normal circumstances, a wound bed will not bleed spontaneously. A wound bleeds in response to some form of trauma to the wound bed.

The trauma may be mechanically induced, eg. by vigorous swabbing or scrubbing of the wound during cleansing. A more common cause of trauma, however, is removal of a dressing that has adhered to the wound bed. The most common culprits are the low adherent dressings, if used as a primary wound dressing.[1] Nurses often attempt to remove adherent dressings by soaking them in water or saline. In the case of low adherent dressings this is successful. The solution lies in a thorough wound assessment enabling the selection of an appropriate dressing which is atraumatic on removal.[2]

A wound may bleed if it has developed a clinical infection: the granulation tissue becomes friable and is easily traumatised.[3]

Bleeding will occur if the nurse undertaking sharp debridement of the wound is unskilled in the technique and debrides beyond the devitalised tissue. This will also be painful for the patient, as well as causing trauma to the wound bed.

A full patient history will indicate whether the patient has any blood clotting disorder or is on anticoagulant therapy, which may produce bleeding in an otherwise healthy wound bed.

A bleeding wound is not a healthy wound, but a traumatised wound. The nurse should ensure that the trauma is not caused by her lack of skill in wound assessment, debridement or choice of dressing product.

1. Thomas S (1994) Low adherence dressings. *J Wound Care* **3**(1): 27–30
2. Williams C (1993) Treating a patient's venous ulcer with a foamed gel dressing. *J Wound Care* **2**(5): 264–5
3. Cutting KF (1994) Criteria for identifying wound infection. *J Wound Care* **3**(4): 198–201

10
All red wounds are healthy

Granulation has the same significance for a tissue viability nurse as red tape has for a marathon runner, namely that the end is in sight. Granulation tissue equates with the formation of a new wound bed. It will fill a cavity, and once up to the level of the surrounding skin will be covered by pale-pink epithelial tissue migrating in from the wound edges. Granulation tissue is so called because of the red granules that are visible in the wound bed. These are the tips of the new blood vessels growing between the spaces of the collagen mesh. These spaces eventually become full and the whole area appears red. Granulation tissue is classically described as red, moist and beefy in appearance. The colour of a wound is a diagnostic tool for identifying tissue type. The classification system is simple, and red tissue is nearly always classed as granulation tissue. It is the simplicity of the system that is both its strength and its weakness, as not all red wounds are composed of healthy granulation tissue.

An infected wound that has reached the granulation stage will not progress any further and the granulation tissue, albeit red, is friable, delicate and breaks down easily.[1]

The dressing or cleansing agent used may alter the colour of the wound bed. Potassium permanganate is used to dry up weeping eczema. It will leave a dark-red/purple stain on the wound and surrounding skin, and will turn nail beds black.

The blood supply to the tissue will alter the shade of the granulation tissue. Arterial impairment produces a pale-red colour, whereas poor venous return results in a dusky-red granulation tissue.[2]

Overgranulation is described as red and beefy, but grows beyond the level of the surrounding skin and is classed as an abnormal healing response. Squamous cell carcinoma can mimic granulation tissue, but differs in its rate of growth and can present as a 'cauliflower' mound on the wound surface.

Certain dermatological conditions present with skin lesions that have red wound beds, eg. pyoderma gangrenosum and epidermolysis bullosa.[3,4]

Consequently, the nurse has to ensure that the wound assessment process is holistic in order to be certain that he/she makes the correct diagnosis when presented with a red wound bed. The clinical appearance alone can be deceptive. The nurse may require the advice of a dermatologist or the results of a tissue biopsy before making a definitive diagnosis.

1.   Harding KG (1990) Wound care: putting theory into clinical practice. *Wounds* **2**(1): 21–32
2.   Bates-Jensen B (1995) Indices to include in wound healing assessment. *Adv Wound Care* **8**(4): 25–33
3.   Samuel J, Williams C (1996) Pyoderma gangrenosum: an inflammatory ulcer. *J Wound Care* **5**(7): 314–18
4.   Fletcher J (1995) Care of a patient with epidermolysis bullosa. *J Wound Care* **4**(1): 20–22

11
Cardiac and respiratory disease do not have an adverse effect on wound healing

Initially one might not expect cardiac and respiratory disease to affect the wound-healing process because of their distance from the wound bed. However, the opposite is true, and despite excellent wound management and pressure relief a wound will not heal if the patient has advanced cardiac or respiratory disease. This is because wounds require oxygenation for healing.

Low tissue oxygen levels at the wound bed indicate that the oxygen is being used up more rapidly than it can be supplied.[1] The wound requires oxygen to heal. Fibroblasts, the cells that stimulate the formation of collagen, which forms the bulk of the new wound bed, require oxygen for collagen synthesis.[2] Once the collagen mesh is formed, angiogenesis occurs and the spaces within the mesh are filled with new blood vessels. This process is also oxygen dependent. Once granulation tissue is formed it will be covered by epithelial tissue, and low oxygen levels slow down the rate of epithelialisation.[3]

Macrophages, which are key players in the wound-healing mechanism, have a high oxygen requirement, especially in the presence of infection. The process of phagocytosis consumes large amounts of oxygen. Consequently, patients with low oxygen delivery to tissues are at greater risk of wound infection.

A patient who is suffering from respiratory disease has a limited ability to inspire sufficient oxygen during respiration. A patient who is suffering from cardiac output problems will be unable to deliver the oxygen to the wound bed, even in the presence of sufficient inspired oxygen. Patients with chronic disease processes will therefore have delayed wound healing.

Patients who have undergone surgery and/or suffered haemorrhage due to trauma will be at added risk from hypovolaemia. Patients who smoke are compromising their ability to oxygenate their tissues. Currently the majority of studies investigating the relationship between low tissue oxygen levels and wound healing have been conducted on animals. There is lack of agreement as to how best to measure tissue oxygen levels. Wound requirements for oxygen vary with the stage of the wound-healing process. More research on the techniques for measuring tissue oxygen tension is required before the optimum level of tissue oxygenation can be established.

1. Hotter A (1984) The physiology and clinical implications of wound healing. *Plast Surg Nurs* **4**(1): 4–13
2. Whitney JD (1990) The influence of tissue oxygen and perfusion on wound healing. *AACN—Clin Issues Crit Care Nurs* **1**(3): 578–84
3. Whitney JD (1989) Physiologic effects of tissue oxygenation on wound healing. *Heart Lung* **18**(5): 466–76

12
Smoking delays wound healing

When a person inhales a cigarette, nicotine is absorbed through the lungs. If a person smokes a cigar or pipe, nicotine is also absorbed via the oral mucosa. Nicotine has a vasoconstrictive effect on tissues, which is enhanced by its ability to prevent vasodilatation. Nicotine also adversely affects the body's immune response and thus its ability to fight wound infection.[1]

Smoking predisposes the arterial walls to injury. Once the arterial walls are damaged, nicotine increases platelet aggregation. The consequent thrombus formation will impede blood flow to the tissues. Wound healing is delayed in smokers, epithelialisation is inhibited and wound contraction is reduced. In animals the amount of necrotic tissue in skin flaps increased when they were exposed to smoke.[2]

The final outcome of wound healing is less cosmetically acceptable in smokers, as their scars are wider.

In conclusion, the reduction in blood flow experienced by smokers may result in delayed wound healing and the formation of wounds due to arterial insufficiency.

1.   Siana JE, Franklid S, Gottrup F (1992) The effect of smoking on tissue function. *J Wound Care* **1**(2): 37–41
2.   Lawrence WT, Murphy RC, Robsob MC (1984) The detrimental effect of cigarette smoking on flap survival. *Br J Plast Surg* **37**: 216–19

13
A wound will only heal when oral steroids are stopped

Steroids are known to have an adverse effect on wound healing. The phases of the wound-healing process that are mainly affected are the first and second phases, ie. the inflammatory and destructive phases. Under normal conditions the inflammatory phase acts as a distress call to the rest of the body. The macrophages respond, and, once at the site of the injury, remove unwanted products, such as bacteria, slough and necrotic tissue. Corticosteroids have an anti-inflammatory action which dampens down the inflammatory response and thus retards wound healing. By reducing the flow of macrophages to the wound bed, steroids place the patient at greater risk of wound infection. A secondary function of macrophages is to stimulate the formation of collagen, the new wound bed, via growth factors. Steroids affect the function of the lysosomes within the macrophage causing it to malfunction.[1] Vitamin A given before wounding can partially counteract the effect of steroids on macrophages.

Ideally, all oral steroid therapy would be stopped for the duration of the time that the patient has a wound. In reality this is not always possible, eg. if the steroids are required for the management of asthma or other respiratory disease. Sometimes it may be possible for the steroid dose to be reduced under medical supervision, to help counteract the adverse effect of the steroid on wound healing.

Steroids may be the primary treatment for certain wounds, such as vasculitic leg ulcers. This type of ulcer results from inflammation of the blood vessel wall which eventually causes occlusion and prevents blood reaching the tissue. Steroids are given to reduce the inflammation in the blood vessels and thus allow the blood to flow and oxygenate the tissues.[2]

Steroids do not stop wound healing but retard the healing process, especially the function of the macrophage. If the patient is on steroid therapy, then the nurse must anticipate a slower healing response and ensure that other factors, eg. nutrition, are enhanced so that the wound has the optimum chance of healing.

1.   Doughty DB (1992) Wound assessment and evaluation and healing. In: Bryant R, ed. *Acute and Chronic Wounds*. Mosby, New York: 31–69
2.   Ertl P (1991) Incidence and aetiology of leg ulcers. *Prof Nurse* **7**(3): 192, 194

14
Nutritional supplements will only aid healing if the patient is underweight

This is a myth. Obese patients have nutritional requirements for wound healing.[1]

A full dietetic assessment along with haematological investigations will reveal the patient's nutritional status. Every patient with a wound should be referred to a dietician for a comprehensive nutritional assessment. Some hospitals have nutritional teams and nutritional nurse specialists are starting to emerge. Within the chain of events the delivery and supervision of the patient's diet may be a weak link. Nutritional assessment is recognised as an essential part of wound care. Catering departments are becoming more flexible and imaginative in their menu formation and in the presentation of patients' meals. Staff shortages and inadequate skill mix may result in insufficient assistance being given to patients who are unable to feed themselves. The reporting of dietary intake is poor if the people who serve and remove patients' meals are not part of the nursing team and are unaware of the value of nutrition or of the cumulative effect of half-eaten meals. How often are ward kitchens full of boxes of dietary supplements that never reach the patients' stomachs ?

There is general consensus on the value of nearly all nutritional components to the wound-healing process. Carbohydrates provide the energy source for the increased cellular activity taking place during wound healing. Fats are an alternative energy source, and fat-soluble vitamins are essential for the building of new cell membranes in wound repair. Protein is essential for building the new wound bed, ie. collagen formation. Protein malnutrition prolongs the inflammatory phase of wound healing and produces weaker wounds. If patients are short of protein before wounding, the effects are worse than if they become depleted of protein after wounding.[2] This highlights the value of providing nutritional support for malnourished patients before surgery.

Vitamins and minerals are essential for effective wound healing. Vitamin A supports epithelial proliferation and consequent migration across granulation tissue. It helps to combat the catabolic effect of glucocorticosteroids and is more efficient if given before wounding. Vitamin B assists formation of the collagen mesh which supports the new blood vessels as they move into the granulating tissue. Vitamin C also assists collagen formation, and together with Vitamin E attacks the damaging oxygen free radicals that are present in infected wounds and during the inflammatory phase of wound healing.

The minerals zinc, copper and iron are required for collagen formation. Zinc is antibacterial, and mainly effective against Gram-positive bacteria. It can be given orally or topically. It is of no benefit if given to raise normal levels — it is only beneficial if zinc levels are low. However, it is notoriously difficult to establish that low levels exist.

The use of vitamin and mineral supplements is contentious. So far they have not been found to be detrimental and are a relatively cheap addition to the patient's wound treatment programme.

Regardless of weight, any patient who has a wound requires nutritional support to enhance the wound-healing process.[3]

1. Pinchcofsky-Devin G (1994) Nutrition and wound healing. *J Wound Care* **3**(5): 231–4
2. Lewis BK, Harding KG (1993) Nutritional intake and wound healing in elderly people. *J Wound Care* **2**(4): 227–9
3. McLaren SMG (1992) Nutrition and wound healing. *J Wound Care* **1**(3): 45–55

15

The deeper the wound the more pain the patient will experience

Pain is a unique phenomenon that is perceived differently by each patient. The amount of pain a patient experiences is dependent upon many factors, not just the depth of the wound.

A suitable method of describing wound pain is sadly lacking. Krasner[1] described three categories of wound pain:

- Non-cyclic acute wound pain — a single episode of acute wound pain, eg. suture removal

- Cyclic acute wound pain — periodic acute wound pain that is present on repeated treatments, eg. at every dressing change

- Chronic wound pain — persistent pain that does not require an external trigger, eg. ischaemic leg pain.

Patients will have a combination of these experiences, depending upon events in the life span of their wound.

Certain wound types are categorised as more painful than others, eg. arterial leg ulcers are more painful than venous leg ulcers. Any breach in the patient's skin has the potential to cause pain. The pain may not be due to the wound but to the position that patients have to adopt as part of their wound management programme, eg. leg elevation or lying on their side if they have osteoarthritis of the hip joints.

A wound does not always produce the level of pain that would be anticipated by its appearance. A grade 5 sacral sore can be pain free, whereas a grade 2 sore, with only epidermal tissue missing, may be agonising for the patient. A study by Ketovuori[2] which examined nurses' perception of surgical wound pain found that nurses who had experienced surgery estimated the intensity of pain lower than those who had no personal experience of the pain, although both groups of nurses estimated the intensity of the pain incorrectly.

Wound pain should not be assessed simply as a question of present or absent, but should be examined more closely. The following aspects should be documented: type, site, nature, severity and frequency of the pain, triggers to the pain and the patient's preferred method of coping with the pain.

There are many strategies for relieving the pain, including both pharmacological and non-pharmacological.[3] An example of the latter is given by Lasoff and McEttrick[4] who highlight the value of allowing children with painful burn wounds to participate in their dressing changes.

Nurses are gatekeepers to analgesia and this puts them in a very powerful position. This situation should be utilised for the benefit of the patient to ensure that their wound history is a pain-free experience.

1.   Krasner D (1995) The chronic wound pain experience: a conceptual model. *Ostomy Wound Manage* **41**(3): 20–25
2.   Ketovuori H (1987) Nurses' and patients' conceptions of wound pain and the administration of analgesics. *J Pain Symptom Manage* **2**(4): 213–18
3.   Kurring P, Young T (1996) A non-pharmacological method of relieving wound pain. *Proceedings of the 6th European Conference on Advances in Wound Management*. Macmillan, London
4.   Lasoff EM, McEttrick MA (1986) Participation versus diversion during dressing change: can nurses' attitudes change? *Issues Compr Pediatr Nurs* **9**(39): 1–8

16
Hypertrophic and keloid are two ways of describing abnormal scarring

The terms hypertrophic and keloid are both used to describe abnormal scarring, but they refer to different types of scars. A hypertrophic scar is raised above the surrounding skin but stays within the confines of the scar tissue. A keloid scar is also raised but extends beyond the original wound.[1]

The physical content of the scars is also different; a biopsy may be required as visually it can be difficult to distinguish between them.

A hypertrophic scar often regresses spontaneously, whereas a keloid scar may not regress and is more disfiguring for the patient. The incidence of keloid scarring is higher in people with darker skin pigmentation. Keloid is usually found in areas of increased skin tension, such as the upper back, anterior chest, shoulders and upper arms. There is a familial tendency for keloid scarring and it has also been associated with endocrine changes.[2] Keloid scars occur as a result of trauma, which may have been surgically induced. They are more likely to develop if the scar is made across Langer's incision lines rather than along them.[3] The treatment for hypertrophic and keloid scars is surgical excision, often accompanied by injection of corticosteroid into the scar.[4] Other suggested treatments include laser therapy, cryotherapy, radiotherapy, pressure garments and silicone gel.[5]

The keloid process is complex and not fully understood, consequently the treatments require further investigation to establish a wholly successful solution to the problem.

1. Murray CJ (1993) Scars and keloids. *Dermatol Clin* **11**(4): 697–707
2. Munro KJG (1995) Hypertrophic and keloid scars. *J Wound Care* **4**(3): 143–8
3. O'Sullivan ST, O'Shaughnessy M, O'Connor TPF (1996) Aetiology and management of hypertrophic scars and keloids. *Ann R Coll Surg Engl* **78**: 168–75
4. Munro KJG (1995) Treatment of hypertrophic and keloid scars. *J Wound Care* **4**(5): 243–5
5. Williams C (1996) Cica-Care: adhesive gel sheet. *Br J Nurs* **4**(14): 875–6

17
Maggots have a place in modern wound management

Maggots were used to clean up war wounds in the First and Second World Wars. Unfortunately the lack of sterility of the maggots resulted in problems of tetanus and gangrene for the patients.

Maggots of the blow-fly species have since been cultured in a sterile environment and used to debride wounds. They are attracted by the smell and presence of decomposing matter. They liquefy and ingest necrotic tissue but not healthy tissue. They destroy bacteria, thereby reducing the amount of infected matter in a wound. The removal of necrotic and infected tissue results in a reduction of odour from the wound bed. Maggots have four requirements for optimum effectiveness: necrotic/infected tissue for food; darkness; moisture; and air.[1] Maggot therapy has been used successfully to treat osteomyelitis and more recently pressure sores.[2] Given the right conditions they can clean a wound within a week, but die once their food source has run out. They are live debriding agents that have the potential to resolve wound infections complicated by antibiotic resistance.

Attitudes of staff and patients may be the main drawback to initiating maggot therapy.

1.   Church JCT (1996) Blow-fly larvae as agents of debridement in chronic infected wounds. *Proceedings of the 5th European Conference on Advances in Wound Management*. European Wound Management Association, Macmillan Magazines, London
2.   Sherman RA, Wyle F, Vulpe M (1995) Maggot therapy for treating pressure ulcers in spinal cord injury patients. *J Spinal Cord Med* **18**(2): 71–4

18
Leeches have a place in modern wound management

Although their use dates back as far as the 19th century, leeches have not been replaced in the field of modern medicine. The medicinal variety of the leech is *Hirudo medicinalis*. It is used to ease venous congestion in compromised tissue. The leech has suckers at both ends of its body. The posterior sucker functions as an anchor and the anterior sucker moves around until it locates a source of food. It feeds upon the blood of mammals, tadpoles, frogs and small fish.[1] The leech has three sharp jaws which contain teeth that pierce the skin of its host. Once the skin is broken the leech secretes an anaesthetic substance to prevent the host detecting the activity and sucking of the leech. It also secretes the enzyme orgelase, which stimulates blood flow to the area. To prevent the blood clotting, the leech secretes hirudin, a short-acting anticoagulant.[2] Leeches can feed for up to two hours and ingest 3–15ml of blood. The leech contains *Aeromonas hydrophila,* a bacterium that helps it to digest the blood. If the leech is not handled with care, there is the risk of it vomiting its contents, which may have been in its stomach for up to 12 months, onto the patient's wound. If this occurs, infection may develop. Abrupt removal of the leech may result in the leech leaving teeth behind in the wound, creating another source of infection. Consequently, antibiotic therapy is given alongside leech therapy as a prophylactic measure.

Clinical conditions that benefit from leech therapy are venous congestion in flap or digit transplants and haematoma formation.[3]

The leech will not outreach to areas with a compromised arterial supply.

There is a risk of blood loss following leech therapy. The anticoagulant may allow the bite site to continue to ooze for 12 hours after removal of the leech.

Patients being considered for leech therapy will require psychological support and written and verbal explanations of the procedure and its anticipated outcome to help them accept this form of therapy.

1.   Peel K (1993) Making sense of leeches. *Nurs Times* **89**(27) 34–5
2.   Caull AF (1993) Using leeches for venous drainage after surgery. *J Wound Care* **2**(5): 294–7
3.   Parker G, Rendell E (1994) Hungry healers. *Nurs Times* **90**(26): 55–8

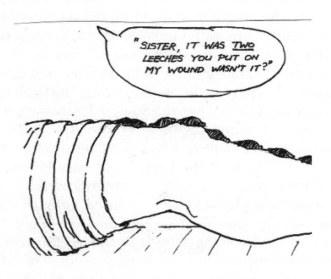

19
Hyperbaric oxygen is a proven aid to wound healing

Hyperbaric oxygen (HBO) therapy requires the patient to inspire 100% oxygen intermittently at a pressure higher than sea level pressure. This is achieved by enclosing the patient in a hyperbaric chamber. Chambers are constructed to accommodate either a single person (monoplace chamber) or a group of people, ie. patients and attendants (multiplace chamber).

There is a vast amount of literature proving the value of HBO in decompression sickness. Research in the field of HBO and wound healing, however, is sadly lacking in both amount and quality. Under normal circumstances 97% of oxygen in the body is transported via haemoglobin and only 0.32% is dissolved in plasma. Under hyperbaric conditions the amount of oxygen dissolved in the plasma is increased. Consequently more oxygen is delivered to the tissues.[1]

In animal studies, HBO therapy is claimed to increase the survival rate of skin flaps. HBO may be beneficial in the management of infected wounds, as the high oxygen pressures in the tissues kill the bacteria. The body's own defences, ie. white blood cells, function more efficiently in a hyperoxygenated environment.

HBO causes vasoconstriction. Although this can restrict the flow of blood to the tissues, the high concentration of oxygen in the blood supply ensures that the supply of oxygen to the tissues remains high. The vasoconstrictive effect prevents the formation of oedema; this effect together with the continued delivery of large amounts of oxygen, makes HBO a suitable therapy for patients with burns or compartment syndrome, where oedema is a problem.

Hammerlund and Sundberg[2] studied the effect of HBO in patients with chronic venous leg ulcers. They found that collagen formation in these patients was increased and recommended HBO as a valuable adjunct to conventional therapy. Arterial and diabetic leg ulcers also responded to HBO.

Some patients, especially those with respiratory problems, are unsuitable for HBO therapy. The most common complication of HBO is barotrauma.

HBO chambers are normally located at naval hospitals and coastal resorts. In America, HBO is a recognised form of treatment for 11 clinical conditions including enhancement of healing in selected problem wounds.

Unfortunately the research does not conclusively prove that HBO aids wound healing. Until proof is available the role of HBO in wound management has to take second place behind research-based practice.

1.   Young T (1995) Hyperbaric oxygen therapy in wound management. *Br J Nurs* **4**(14): 796–803
2.   Hammerlund C, Sundberg T (1994) Hyperbaric oxygen reduced size of chronic leg ulcers: a randomised double-blind study. *Plast Reconstr Surg* **93**(4): 829–33

20
To leave a wound undisturbed for one week is clinically negligent

The nurse, under the Code of Professional Conduct, has a legal and professional duty to care for patients. The nurse is professionally accountable to the United Kingdom Central Council for Nursing, Midwifery and Health Visiting, contractually accountable to her employer, and legally accountable for her actions.

A nurse could be found negligent if she failed in her care of a patient and as a consequence the patient suffered harm. Professionally a nurse could be found guilty of misconduct for the same reason, even if the patient did not come to any harm.[1]

If patients claimed that they suffered negligent treatment, their claim would be based upon the fact that, as a result of nurses' intervention, they spent unnecessary time in hospital and suffered unnecessary physical and financial harm as a consequence.[2] Patients would have to prove that the treatment of their condition fell below the standard expected of reasonably competent practitioners in their respective fields.[3] Reasonable can be ascertained by establishing whether the decision would be supported by a responsible body of nurses in the relevant specialty.

The negligence may arise out of a failure to act or a lack of professional knowledge. Nursing negligence in relation to tissue viability can result from adherence to traditional methods, rather than basing practice on research.[4] Wound care crosses all nursing specialties consequently most nurses should have a sound knowledge of wound assessment, healing and management. Research that has an impact on wound healing today was first published in 1962,[5] and the volume of literature on the subject has continued to expand ever since.

Leaving a wound undisturbed for a week could be viewed as excellent wound management practice, if the rationale was clear and based upon research, and the assessment and treatment plans were documented clearly and accurately. An example of this would be the use of a hydrocolloid dressing to debride a necrotic wound. However, leaving a wet soggy gauze dressing on an infected wound for a week would fall below a reasonable standard, and the patient would undoubtedly suffer as a result.

1. United Kingdom Central Council for Nursing, Midwifery and Health Visiting (1996) *Guidelines for Professional Practice.* UKCC, London
2. Tingle J (1992) Some legal issues in wound management. *Nurs Stand* **6**(34 Suppl): 4–5
3. Bennett G, Moody M (1995) *Wound Care for Health Professionals.* Chapman and Hall, London
4. Moody M (1992) Accountability in wound management. *Nurs Stand* **6**(23 Suppl): 10–11
5. Winter GD (1962) Formation of the scab and rate of epithelialisation of superficial wounds in the skin of the young domestic pig. *Nature* **193**: 293–4

CHAPTER TWO
WOUND CLEANSING/
WOUND INFECTION

1

A wound bed should be free from bacteria to allow healing to take place

To attempt to eradicate all bacteria from a wound is unrealistic, and virtually impossible to achieve.

Various topical agents claim to reduce bacterial levels within wounds.[1] This could be seen as an effective therapeutic intervention if the level of bacteria that can be present in a wound and healing still take place were known. Unfortunately, this information is not available; what is known is that wounds do not have to be sterile or free from bacteria to heal.[2] The presence of bacteria in a wound bed stimulates an inflammatory response, resulting in an improved blood supply to the wound and the arrival of neutrophils and macrophages at the wound bed. In most cases, these cells are able to achieve a balance between colonisation and infection. Wound exudate is beneficial to the wound-healing process and is actively bactericidal.

White blood cells function most effectively under an occlusive dressing. Therefore, rather than attempting to unnecessarily eradicate bacteria from a wound, the nurse should aim to provide an occlusive environment at the wound bed that will facilitate wound healing and allow the body's natural defences to work to their maximum potential.

1. Williams C (1995) Iodosorb and Iodoflex. *Br J Nurs* **4**(5): 283–4
2. Phillips E, Young T (1996) Methicillin-resistant *Staphylococcus aureus* and wound management. *Br J Nurs* **4**(22): 1345–9

2

All wound exudate should be removed to speed up wound healing

The visual appearance of wound exudate can be quite alarming for the patient and the nurse. It can present as a green/brown soggy dressing following liquefaction of slough and necrotic tissue from the wound bed. After surgical debridement it may be bloody and provoke fears of haemorrhage. If the wound is granulating and healing it will appear as a pale-pink/yellow fluid. The exudate can take on the appearance of the cleansing agent or dressing product, eg. the dark-red/brown of potassium permanganate or the amber of hydrocolloid dressings.

In the early days of film dressings the exudate that collected under the dressing was removed by aspiration. Today, if the volume of exudate is moderate/heavy, a film dressing would not be the dressing of choice. Perhaps it was the early practice of draining exudate that led nurses to believe that its presence was detrimental to the wound bed. This is a myth: the presence of wound exudate is beneficial to the wound bed.

Chen *et al*[1] examined the exudate from full- and partial-thickness pig wounds covered with an occlusive dressing. They discovered that it was essential to retain exudate at the wound bed as it contained substances that stimulated the formation of granulation tissue and the activation of growth factors required to orchestrate the wound-healing process.

In an animal study, white blood cells in the wound exudate were found to be as effective at killing bacteria as those in circulating blood. Wound exudate therefore has a major role to play in eliminating wound infection.[2]

The exudate under hydrocolloid dressings used to treat burn wounds has been found to increase cell growth.[3]

Wound exudate plays an important role in the wound-healing process and should not be removed from the wound bed. In infected wounds or wounds with large surface areas, copious amounts of wound exudate will be produced. In these situations the excess exudate should be removed to prevent maceration of the surrounding skin, leaving sufficient fluid in the wound bed to enhance the wound-healing process.

1. Chen WYJ, Rogers AA, Lyden MJ (1992) Characterization of biologic properties of wound fluid collection during early stages of wound healing. *J Invest Dermatol* **99**(5): 559–64
2. Hohn DC, Ponce B, Burton RW, Hunt TK (1977) Anti-microbial systems of the surgical wound. A comparison of oxidative metabolism and microbicidal capacity of phagocytes from wounds and from peripheral blood. *Am J Surg* **133**: 597–600
3. Madden MR, Nolan E, Finklestein JL *et al* (1989) Comparison of an occlusive and semi occlusive dressing and the effect of the wound exudate upon keratinocyte proliferation. *J Trauma* **29**(7): 924–31

3
Keeping a wound warm will increase the number of bacteria and delay healing

One of the properties of an ideal dressing is that it should keep the wound bed warm. All wounds contain bacteria, and the thought of providing them with a warm environment can engender fears of inducing wound infection in some nurses. This fear can now be dispelled following a review of the literature by Hutchinson and Lawrence[1] who concluded that: 'The rate of clinical infection is lower under occlusion than when non-occlusive dressings are used; this is likely to be a result of normal activity of the host defences under occlusive dressings.'

The process of redressing a wound and the consequent exposure of the wound bed can slow down the wound-healing process. A study of 420 patients during dressing changes found that it took 40 minutes for the wounds to return to body temperature and three hours for the white blood cells at the wound bed to recommence functioning. Bearing in mind that body temperature is 37°C, extended exposure of wet wounds may reduce the temperature to 12°C. The use of a cold cleansing agent has the potential to reduce the temperature even further to 3°C.[2] Animal studies have demonstrated an increase in the formation of epidermal tissue under a film dressing owing to the increase in temperature.[3]

Hermans[4] identified the thermal value of an occlusive dressing. The temperature of a wound bed under a non-occlusive dressing is 25–27°C and under a hydrocolloid dressing is 32.7–35.2°C. Non-occlusion causes the evaporation of exudate, which in turn cools the wound bed and eventually leads to dehydration of the wound.

The provision of warmth at the wound bed may increase the number of bacteria, but provided that it takes place under an occlusive/semi-occlusive dressing it should not have a detrimental effect on wound healing.

1. Hutchinson JJ, Lawrence JC (1991) Wound infection under occlusive dressings. *J Hosp Infect* **17**: 83–94
2. Myers JA(1982) Modern plastic surgical dressings. *Health Soc Serv J* **92**(4788): 336–7
3. Lock P (1980) The effects of temperature on mitotic activity at the edge of experimental wounds. In: Lundgren A, Soner AB, eds. *Symposia on Wound Healing: Plastic, Surgical and Dermatologic Aspects*. Molndal, Sweden: 103–7
4. Hermans MHE (1993) Air exposure versus occlusion: merits and disadvantages of different dressings. *J Wound Care* **2**(6): 362–5

4

A smelly wound is an infected wound

Wounds produce various smells, some of them normal and some abnormal. The abnormal smells are usually caused by the decomposition of dead flesh, ie. necrotic tissue. In these wounds it is the diamines, cadaverine and putrescine, that cause the odour.[1] Therefore when the offending tissue is debrided, the smell will disappear. A secondary cause of odour is a wet soggy dressing left on a patient's wound. Dressings should be changed as soon as they become wet, as bacteria readily penetrate wet dressings.[2] Although in both cases the smell is often offensive, it does not mean that it is caused by a wound infection, the smell being localised to the offensive tissue/dressing.

This issue is complicated by the fact that infected wounds are also smelly. However, with infected wounds the smell occurs suddenly, does not disappear following debridement of the necrotic tissue, and is accompanied by an increase in wound exudate. The wound bed may start to bleed and suddenly begin to deteriorate. Consequently smell alone is not diagnostic of wound infection; such a diagnosis requires, in addition, a detailed examination of the wound bed, its surrounding skin and general progress. To subject a patient to antibiotic therapy on the grounds of odour alone will not aid the wound-healing process. Certain types of dressings can assist in combating wound odour.[3,4]

1. Haughton WC, Young T (1995) Common problems in wound care: malodorous wounds. *Br J Nurs* **4**(16): 959–63
2. Ayliffe GAJ, Lowbury EJL, Geddes AM, Williams JD (1992) *Control of Hospital Infection. A Practical Handbook*. 3rd edn. Chapman & Hall Medical, London
3. Williams C (1994) Actisorb Plus. *Br J Nurs* **3**(15): 786–8
4. Williams C (1996) Lyofoam. *Br J Nurs* **5**(12): 757–9

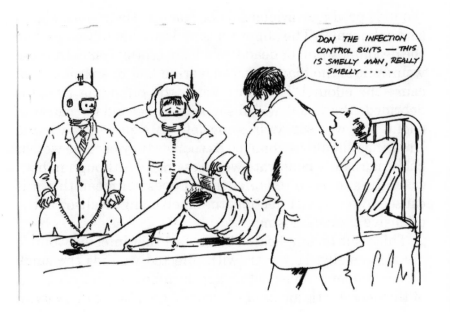

5
Erythema around the wound edges is confirmation of wound infection

Erythema is defined as an area of red tissue and is often present during an acute inflammatory response. The inflammatory response may be stimulated by many factors: infection, foreign bodies, ischaemia, and pressure or trauma to the wound bed.

It is often difficult to distinguish between erythema that is infective in origin and erythema due to other causes. A patient who has a sacral pressure sore may have a red area around the sore that is pressure induced. Erythema may be the first sign of pressure sore formation.[1] The redness around a sacral sore may also be caused by maceration from urine, faeces or wound exudate.

Patients with lower limb arterial disease may present with a red leg despite peripheral ischaemia.

Erythema that is infective in origin is caused by local vasodilatation and is hot to the touch. Patients with a systemic infection will, in most cases, also exhibit a pyrexia and have a generalised increase in body temperature. If the wound is managed by occlusion or a foam dressing, the thermal properties of the dressing may also produce a local increase in the wound bed temperature. Consequently, an increase in the temperature of the skin surrounding the wound may be difficult to detect.[2]

The erythema should be mapped, either on the patient's skin or on a wound-mapping grid, to establish its spread.

The complexities indicate that erythema alone is an unreliable indicator of wound infection.

1.   Young T (1996) Classification of pressure sores. *Br J Nurs* **5**(7): 438–46
2.   Cutting K (1994) Detecting infection. *Nurs Times* **90**(5): 60–2

~ms identified on a wound swab require antibiotic therapy

The results of a wound swab require a decision to treat or not to treat. This decision can be assisted by providing the laboratory staff with a full clinical picture of the problem, otherwise they have to work blind. They will require the following details:

Swab — not just the wound, but also the site and type/cause of the wound, eg. pressure sore, venous leg ulcer.

Antibiotic treatment — not just yes or no, but type, duration of treatment and prior treatment.

Description — sudden alterations within the wound bed, eg. bleeding, amount of wound exudate, type and colour of wound exudate, type of tissue in the wound bed, colour of surrounding skin, presence of pyrexia and/or tachycardia.

This information will assist the laboratory staff in their deliberations and result in the provision of more accurate data for clinical interpretation. The full picture will assist in recognising problems, eg. *Escherichia coli* that is normally resident in the bowel would not be remarkable if identified in a sacral pressure sore, but significant if found in a facial trauma wound.

A swab taken from any part of the body would produce a list of commensal bacteria, and it would be ridiculous to treat these. Treatment is only necessary if the patient has a systemic infection. Otherwise there exists the potential for the development of antibiotic resistance, and for the patient to suffer unnecessarily from the side-effects of the antibiotics, eg. nausea and diarrhoea.

Sometimes antibiotic therapy is prescribed prophylactically, eg. for patients undergoing cardiac, implant or orthopaedic surgery.

A wound swab report showing the presence of bacteria in the wound bed is not alone sufficient to warrant antibiotic therapy. If the patient has a systemic infection, then antibiotics should probably be prescribed. If the bacteria have colonised the wound, and are not causing a systemic response, then antibiotic therapy is inappropriate.

7
Topical antibiotics should not be used for treating infected wounds

This is not a myth but sound clinical practice. If a patient has a wound infection that presents as a systemic infection, then systemic (oral) not topical antibiotics should be prescribed. Historically, clinicians have attempted to eradicate wound infection by applying antibiotics topically to the wound bed. If the wound bed is covered with slough or necrotic tissue the antibiotic will not be able to penetrate the tissue.[1] The practice of applying topical antibiotics has largely disappeared because of concerns about the occurrence of sensitivity reactions at the wound site, and the emergence of resistant strains of bacteria.[2] Unfortunately, antibiotic-impregnated tulles are still available on prescription and thus their use continues, even though their efficacy in the treatment of infected wounds has not been proven.[3]

Topical preparations of metronidazole are promoted in the management of fungating wounds. This agent is an excellent deodoriser and the problems of sensitivity and resistance are secondary to the patient's diagnosis and wound management problems. Kallehave *et al*[4] report six cases of successful treatment of complicated, infected soft tissue wounds with wound sponges impregnated with collagen and/or gentamicin, although they state that, in common with other centres, they have a general policy of not using antibiotics topically on wounds.

Complex wounds and the emergence of antibiotic-resistant strains of bacteria are producing challenges for wound management. However there is no evidence, so far, that the use of topical antibiotics is beneficial in the treatment of infected wounds.

1. Doughty DB (1992) In: Bryant RA, ed. *Acute and Chronic Wounds: Nursing Management.* Mosby, New York
2. Thomas S (1990) *Wound Management and Dressings.* The Pharmaceutical Press, London
3. Leaper DJ (1994) Prophylactic and therapeutic role of antibiotics in wound care. *Am J Surg* **167**(1A Suppl): 15s–20s
4. Kallehave F, Moesgard F, Gottrup F (1996) Topical antibiotics used in the treatment of complex wounds. *J Wound Care* **5**(4): 158–60

No 8
Antiseptics do not harm wounds

Antiseptic solutions are used to enhance the wound-cleansing process and reduce the number of bacteria at the wound bed. A variety of antiseptics are used in various guises for wound cleansing, including chlorhexidine, iodine, acetic acid, potassium permanganate and proflavine.

For each of the antiseptics, research can be found to promote or reject its use in wound healing. There is no doubt that antiseptics have the ability to kill a wide range of bacteria. The question should not be are they effective, but are they required in the first place? Open wounds do not have to be sterile to heal.[1] It is commonly claimed that antiseptics are inactivated by the presence of blood, pus and slough. Wounds without these features are probably clean and granulating and therefore in no need of antiseptic therapy.

The following detrimental effects of antiseptics on wounds have been recorded. Povidone-iodine 1% and 0.25% acetic acid are cytotoxic to cultured human fibroblasts.[2] Povidone-iodine 10% and chlorhexidine 0.05% with cetrimide are toxic to fibroblasts, reducing their ability to produce collagen, which is necessary for the formation of granulation tissue.[3]

Within the area of tissue viability there exists two camps: the antiseptic users and the non-antiseptic users. To date, the mass of literature has not helped in reconciling their opinions. It is difficult to form an opinion in the presence of such diverse views and often weak supporting literature, but an adage of Rodeheaver[4] is always a good guide: 'Don't put into a wound what you wouldn't put into your eye.'

1. Leaper D (1994) Prophylactic and therapeutic role of antibiotics in wound care. *Am J Surg* **167**(1A Suppl): 15s–20s
2. Lineaweaver W, Howard R, Soucy D *et al* (1985) Topical antimicrobial toxicity. *Arch Surg* **120**: 267–70
3. Cameron S, Leaper D (1988) Antiseptic toxicity in open wounds. *Nurs Times* **84**(25): 77
4. Rodeheaver G (1989) Controversies in topical wound management. *Wounds* **1**(1): 19–27

9
Salt baths have an important role to play in reducing wound infection

This is a myth. Salt is often thought to have antibacterial properties and is therefore used as a bath additive for patients with infected wounds. The literature does not support this practice. A study of the methods of achieving disinfection in bath water found that the addition of 250g of salt to a bath of water had no antibacterial effect.[1] Previously, a tub of salt could be found in all hospital bathrooms, issued by pharmacy departments, which gave a false impression of official endorsement of the product.

The addition of salt to bath water is thought to provide an isotonic solution. However, this is extremely difficult to achieve. Are nurses aware of the volume of water in a bath, and the correct amount of salt required per litre of water? In a personal communication, an infection control nurse stated that Lucozade™ is promoted for its isotonic properties, but, like the salt bath, is not recommended for wound cleansing![2]

A study by Sleep and Grant[3] compared the use of salt, Savlon™ and plain water for the treatment of the perineum in the post-partum period. There was no statistical difference between the treatments in relation to pain relief and wound healing. The authors found no reason to support the routine use of salt baths.

It is a lay belief that salt has healing properties. The value of choice and respect for patients' beliefs should be acknowledged. Austin[4] highlighted the psychological benefits of salt baths, even when nurses were aware of the lack of research to substantiate the practice. Perhaps in these situations the patient should be made aware of the lack of evidence, and then be allowed to make an informed choice. The problem arises when the nurse is not aware of the background and encourages a practice that is one of the myths of wound management.

1. Ayliffe GAJ, Babb JR, Collins BJ (1975) Disinfection of baths and bath water. *Nurs Times* **71**(37): 22–3
2. Kiernan M (1996) Infection control and wound management. Personal communication
3. Sleep J, Grant A (1988) Effects of salt and Savlon bath concentrate post-partum. *Nurs Times* **84**(21): 55–7
4. Austin L (1988) The salt bath myth. *Nurs Times* **84**(9): 79–83

10
Bathing with an open wound is an unsafe practice

If a patient has a sacral pressure sore and is incontinent of urine and/or faeces, there is a high chance that the wound will become contaminated on a daily basis. It is extremely difficult to remove faeces from a sacral wound using the irrigation method of wound cleansing. Often the irrigation is replaced by swabbing to remove the faeces from the wound bed. If the sore is a cavity it is almost impossible to inspect the area visually to ensure that all the faeces have been removed. The issue is compounded by patient problems such as confusion or paralysis, resulting in the patient being unaware that contamination has occurred. In these situations a sensible option would be to give the patient a warm bath.[1] This would not only facilitate wound cleansing, but also make the patient feel clean and therefore less likely to complain 'nurse, I'm dirty' — a common cry in hospitals today. The patient would hopefully be maintaining standards and a level of dignity that he/she would achieve if well enough to do so independently.

The issue of safety would arise if there was a risk of infection being transmitted either to or from the patient. If the patient does not have a wound infection then it is acceptable to clean the bath after use with a general purpose detergent. If the patient does have an infection, eg. methicillin-resistant *Staphylococcus aureus*, he/she will probably be on a daily skin decontamination regimen, and be bathed daily. The bath/shower should be cleaned with hypochloride solution.

In America, hydrotherapy is often advocated as a method of wound cleansing. This is administered via a whirlpool on a daily basis. The rationale is that the turbulence will help to remove superficial debris from the wound. It is not recommended for granulating wounds, as the turbulence could traumatise the delicate tissue.[2]

1. Young T (1995) Common problems in wound care: wound cleansing. *Br J Nurs* **4**(5): 286–9
2. Feedar JA, Kloth LC (1990) In: Kloth LC, McCulloch JM, Feedar JA. *Wound Healing: Alternatives in Management*. FA Davis, Philadelphia

11
Hydrogen peroxide can help to clean traumatic wounds

Hydrogen peroxide can assist in cleaning a traumatic wound that contains visible debris, eg. grit and soil. If the debris is left *in situ*, it can produce ugly scars, often referred to as tattooing.

Hydrogen peroxide is only effective for a short period of time, ie. when it is effervescing. During this period of activity it is oxidising and liberating oxygen as it decomposes. It is broken down by the enzyme catalase, which is found in all living tissue.[1] The mechanical effect of the bubbling dislodges the debris in the wound. The alteration in the wound environment caused by the oxidation stops the multiplication of aerobic bacteria by liberating all the available oxygen. Hydrogen peroxide is also thought to have an antiviral action.[2]

Problems exist with the use of hydrogen peroxide in wound cleansing. If the solution is used in a closed cavity, there is a risk of gas embolism forming.[3] Hydrogen peroxide is inactivated by slough, blood and pus, and is therefore not indicated for wounds containing these substances. If hydrogen peroxide continues to be used after the cleansing is complete, it can produce blistering in the new epithelial tissue.

Hydrogen peroxide can be used to dislodge debris in traumatic wounds, but its use should be restricted to this situation. Extended use puts the wound-healing process at risk of the general problems associated with topical antiseptic therapy.

1. Thomas S (1990) *Wound Management and Dressings*. The Pharmaceutical Press, London
2. Stewart A, Foster M, Leaper D (1985) Cleaning versus healing. *Community Outlook* **August**: 23–6
3. Morison MJ (1990) Wound cleansing: which solution ? *Nurs Stand* 4(52): 4–6

12
Debridement is a method of wound cleansing

Debridement is defined by Dealey[1] as the removal of necrotic or devitalised tissue from the wound by surgical or chemical means or by autolysis. It does, therefore constitute a method of wound cleansing. Healing cannot proceed fully in the presence of devitalised tissue, which also provides a haven and breeding ground for bacteria. Kloth[2] distinguishes between selective and non-selective debridement, where non-selective debridement removes both viable and non-viable tissue and also causes trauma to granulating tissue.

The quickest method of debridement is sharp debridement. The tissue is excised completely, usually under general anaesthetic. Poston[3] suggests that competent, experienced and knowledgeable nurses should undertake a lesser form of sharp debridement when the devitalised tissue is found just above the level of viable tissue. Caution is always advocated in patients with clotting disorders or who have prostheses or devices *in situ*.

Chemical debridement involves the application of enzymatic preparations to the necrotic tissue. Their method of application and frequency of reapplication have led to a decline in their popularity.[4]

Autolysis is the body's own method of removing devitalised tissue. The macrophage is the key player in this process, and works most effectively in a warm environment. Consequently, autolysis is hastened by the application of wound dressings that provide a wet and warm environment, eg. hydrogels and hydrocolloids.[5,6]

All the above are selective methods of debridement. A non-selective method is reported in the American literature and consists of a wet-to-dry regimen.[7] Wet wide-mesh gauze is applied to the wound bed and allowed to dry out and adhere to the tissue. It is then forcibly removed, and during the process any tissue that has stuck to the gauze is also removed. The problem is that the process is painful for the patient and good tissue is debrided along with the necrotic tissue.

Although the methods have been categorised separately, in reality the nurse will often utilise several methods of debridement during the life span of a wound. The choice of debridement technique should ensure a speedy and atraumatic cleansing of the wound bed.

1. Dealey C (1994) *The Care of Wounds*. Blackwell Scientific, Oxford
2. Kloth LC, McCulloch JM, Feedar JA (1990) *Wound Healing: Alternatives in Management*. FA Davis, Philadelphia
3. Poston J (1996) Sharp debridement of devitalised tissue: the nurse's role. *Br J Nurs* **5**(11): 655–62
4. Thomas S (1994) Wound cleansing agents. *J Wound Care* **3**(7): 325–8
5. Williams C (1994) Granuflex. *Br J Nurs* **3**(14): 730–3
6. Williams C (1996) Granugel: hydrocolloid gel. *Br J Nurs* **5**(3): 188–90
7. Fowler E, Van Rijswijk L (1995) Using wound debridement to help achieve goals of care. *Ostomy Wound Manage* **41**(7a Suppl): 23s–25s

13
Wounds should be cleansed at every dressing change

The aim of wound cleansing is to remove contaminated/foreign material from the wound bed. The materials that fulfil these criteria and can be found within a wound bed are slough, necrotic tissue, exudate and dressing debris.[1]

If any of the above are present, the nurse has to decide whether they can be removed by cleansing or whether debridement (autolytic, manual or enzymatic) is a more appropriate method of removal.

If the wound is clean and granulating, wound cleansing is not required. Wound cleansing would be an unnecessary addition to the redressing procedure. Unfortunately, nurses often open the dressing pack and prepare the wound cleansing solution before completing the wound assessment, and then, in order to prevent waste, proceed to cleanse the wound. This is ritualistic practice that will not facilitate wound healing. It will only delay the dressing of the wound.[2] There is also the risk of traumatising the new tissue during the cleansing process. The granulation tissue can be preserved in prime condition by a non-interventionist approach to wound cleansing. In this instance the only requirement is for dressing renewal. If the wound does not need cleansing then don't clean it!

1.   Cutting K F (1990) Wound cleansing. *Surg Nurse* **3**(3): 4–8
2.   Johnson A (1988) The cleansing ethic. *Community Outlook* **February**: 9–10

14
A sterile procedure is necessary for all wound cleansing situations

The reason for using a sterile/aseptic procedure for wound cleansing is protection. At one time the aim would have been solely to protect the patient from the risk of cross-infection, with the nurse being the main carrier of potential pathogens. Today the nurse also requires protection, especially from viral transmission that occurs via body fluids.[1] The aseptic procedure itself is a task-oriented approach that is surrounded by myths. It requires the nurse to have the manual dexterity of Edward Scissorhands to use the forceps, and the memory of a mastermind contestant to recall which are the clean and which are the dirty forceps. The farce of this procedure has long been recognised and, thankfully, very few dressing packs today contain forceps; most now contain sterile gloves.

Whether or not an aseptic procedure is used depends on the level of risk to the patient. Patients who are immunocompromised or who have undergone surgery involving prosthetic implants are considered to be at high risk of developing postoperative infective complications. Consequently this group of patients should always be subject to asepsis during the wound-cleansing procedure.

Patients with chronic wounds, eg. pressure sores and venous leg ulcers that are colonised with bacteria, are frequently subjected to clean rather than aseptic procedures during wound cleansing.[2] No guidelines exist for a clean procedure. The main differences between a clean procedure and an aseptic procedure are as follows:

Detail	Aseptic	Clean
Venue	Dressing room with air flow Ward cleaning ceased for 30 minutes and curtains drawn for 10 minutes before procedure commences	At bedside
Solution	Sterile water/saline	Tap water
Gloves	Yes	Yes/no
Dressing trolley	Cleaned at the beginning of the day and top wiped with 70% alcohol between each dressing change	Bowl/bath If leg ulcer use bucket and bin liner
Apron	Yes	Yes

There is no need to use an aseptic procedure for every dressing change; individual patient assessment will dictate whether a clean or aseptic procedure is required.

1.   Ayliffe GAJ, Lowbury EJL, Geddes A M, Williams JD (1992) *Control of Hospital Infection: A Practical Handbook*. 3rd edn. Chapman & Hall Medical, London
2.   Morison MJ (1989) Wound cleansing — which solution? *Prof Nurse* **4**(5): 220–5

No 15
Swabbing with gauze or cotton wool is the best method of cleansing a wound

No it is not! Swabbing a wound involves the application of pressure to the wound bed. This is often completed forcefully in an attempt to remove slough/necrotic tissue that is firmly adherent to the wound bed, and therefore not ripe for removal. Several different swabbing techniques are utilised. In a study of three techniques Thomlinson[1] found that no single technique was superior and that all three just redistributed the organisms on the wound surface. The irrigation method is thought to be less damaging to the wound bed.[2]

The amount of force required to remove contaminated material from the wound bed is thought to be 6–8 psi. This can be achieved using a 35ml syringe and a 19 gauge needle.[3] Madden *et al*[4] specified that a higher psi of 25 was necessary to remove bacteria from a wound. While this may be true, a high pressure could also traumatise granulation tissue.

Aerosol cans containing saline are now available for wound cleansing. They are convenient and easy to use.[5,7]

If the irrigation method of cleansing is chosen, there is no need for gauze or cotton wool. If swabbing is necessary then non-woven swabs are preferable as they will shed less fibres into the wound than cotton wool.[6] The fibres will be viewed as a foreign body and induce an inflammatory response in the wound bed. They may also be a source of infection or cause a newly healed wound to break down.

1.   Thomlinson D (1987) To clean or not to clean? *Nurs Times* **83**(9): 71–5
2.   Glide S (1992) Cleaning choices. *Nurs Times* **88**(19): 74–8

3.   Stevenson TR, Thacker JG, Rodeheaver G, Bacchetta C, Edgerton MT, Edlish RF (1976) Cleansing the traumatic wound by high pressure irrigation. *J Am Coll Emerg Phys* **5**(1): 17–21
4.   Madden J, Richard BA, Edlich F *et al* (1971) Application of the principles of fluid dynamics to surgical wound irrigation. *Curr Top Surg Res* **3**: 85–93
5.   Williams C (1996) Irriclens: a sterile wound cleanser in an aerosol can. *Br J Nurs* **5**(16): 1008–10
6.   Thomas S, Loveless P, Heyn P, Toyick N (1993) Comparing non woven, filmated and woven gauze swabs. *J Wound Care* **2**(1): 35–41
7.   Chisholm CD, Cordell WH, Rogers K, Woods JR (1992) Comparison of a new pressurized saline canister versus syringe irrigation for laceration cleansing in the emergency department. *Ann Emerg Med* **21**(11): 1364–7

16
Poor surgical technique is the most common cause of wound breakdown

Poor surgical technique commonly leads to wound infection and thus wound breakdown. There are a multitude of factors that put a patient at risk of developing a wound infection.[1] They may be summarised as follows:

PATIENT	Immunological status
ENVIRONMENT	Preoperative skin preparation
	Length of preoperative stay
	Antibiotic therapy
	Theatre air flow system
SURGERY	Surgeon
	Skin closure technique and materials
	Duration of the surgery
	Anatomical site of the surgery
	Wound drainage
	Type of operation which can be classified as:
	— clean (non-traumatic or non-infected)
	— clean contaminated (involving bronchi, gastrointestinal or genitourinary tract)
	— contaminated (traumatic wounds)
	— dirty (involving old wounds, abscesses or perforated viscera)

There is no doubt that the input of the surgeon is a major factor in the development of wound infection. However, there is no evidence that the surgeon's input is the only major risk factor,[2] although feedback on wound infection rates to surgeons can result in a reduction in the number of infected wounds.[3] Methods to control the risk of wound infection appear to be successful in clean operations, but their effectiveness decreases as the level of contamination rises.

When comparing data to identify a common cause of wound infection, the main problem is that there is no exact definition of a wound infection.[4] This prevents direct comparisons being made and the major factors being identified.

1.   Ayliffe GAJ, Lowbury EJL, Geddes AM, Williams JD (1992) *Control of Hospital Infection. A Practical Handbook*. 3rd edn. Chapman & Hall Medical, London
2.   Cruse PSE, Foord RA (1980) A ten year prospective study of 62,939 surgical wounds. *Surg Clin N Am* **60**(1): 27–40
3.   Mishnki SF, Jeffery PJ, Law DJW (1992) Wound infection: the surgeon's responsibility. *J Wound Care* **1**(2): 32–6
4.   Briggs M (1996) Epidemiological methods in the study of surgical wound infection. *J Wound Care* **5**(4): 186–91

17
Shaving patients before surgery will reduce postoperative wound infection rates

This is a myth. Shaving actually increases surgical wound infection rates. Initially it was thought that hair harboured bacteria, and that if it was not removed bacteria would pass into the wound and cause infection. All hair in close proximity to the operation site was therefore removed.

Infection may occur following shaving with a safety razor because shaving causes tiny cuts in the skin. The cuts become a reservoir for bacteria and thus increase the risk of postoperative infection. Alternative methods of removing hair include electric hair clippers and depilatory cream. Clippers still cause trauma to the skin, but the degree of trauma is less than that caused by razors.[1] Clippers are difficult to clean and must be cleaned between patients. Creams are less traumatic to the skin than razors or clippers. Creams can be messy to use, and some patients may have an adverse reaction to them. Patch testing before use is therefore recommended. As far back as 1980, a link was demonstrated between shaving and postoperative infection rates, as follows:

Infection rate   2.5% — patients shaved with a safety razor
                               1.7% — patients shaved with hair clippers
                               1.4% — patients shaved with electric razor
                               0.9% — patients not shaved or clipped

Preoperative shaving still appears to be a ritualistic practice in many areas.[2] Often the problem is not an inability to obtain depilatory creams, but difficulty in altering the attitudes of doctors and nurses to preoperative shaving. If the practice of shaving cannot be eliminated, the risk of postoperative wound infection is reduced if shaving is done as near to the time of operation as possible.

1.   Freshwater D (1992) Pre-operative preparation of skin. A review of the literature. *Surg Nurse* **5**(5): 6–10
2.   Flanagan M, Fletcher J, Hollingworth H (1994) Pre-op shaving (readers' questions). *J Wound Care* **3**(7): 388

18
Patients with methicillin-resistant *Staphyloccocus aureus* (MRSA) in their wounds should be nursed in an isolation cubicle

MRSA is a bacterium that lives on human skin and thrives in the nose, axilla, groin and perineum. It is a commensal and does not cause a problem unless it is offered a portal of entry into the underlying tissues. A wound is an ideal portal of entry. Once present in a wound, the bacterium may colonise the wound or increase in sufficient numbers to cause a systemic infection.

MRSA is a form of *Staphylococcus aureus* that has developed resistance to the following antibiotics: erythromycin, gentamicin, penicillin, tetracycline, ciprofloxacin, fusidic acid, kanamycin and rifampicin. There are only a few antibiotics that are successful in treating infections caused by MRSA. The main one is vancomycin, which is expensive and has to be administered intravenously.

Certain strains of MRSA are able to spread quickly between patients. These are epidemic strains and are referred to as EMRSA.

A patient who has MRSA in his/her wound and is also a hospital inpatient should be nursed in isolation until the strain is identified and treated.[1] In the community, if the patient is colonised but not infected with MRSA, then he/she can share a room with other residents, provided that the other residents do not have open wounds.[2]

The period of isolation can be decreased by the use of hydrocolloid wound dressings.[3] These dressings have been proven to keep the MRSA *in situ* in the wound and thus reduce the risk of cross-infection.[4]

1. Duckworth G (1990) Revised guidelines for the control of epidemic MRSA. *J Hosp Infect* **16**: 351–77

2. Duckworth G, Heathcock R (1995) Guidelines on the control of MRSA in the community. *J Hosp Infect* **31**: 1–12
3. Young T (1996) MRSA. *J Wound Care* **5**(10): 475–7
4. Wilson P, Burroughs D, Dunn LJ (1988) MRSA and hydrocolloid dressings. *Pharm J* **241**(6513): 787–8

No 19
Human immuno deficiency virus (HIV) cannot be contracted via wound exudate

To date there are no recorded cases of HIV being contracted by health care personnel from wound exudate. However, this does not mean that there is no potential for transmission. The virus and its method of transmission have to be examined to establish whether there is the possibility of transmission via wound exudate. There are three primary modes of HIV transmission: sexual contact, perinatally and exposure to blood. Universal precautions, if adhered to, protect both the patient and the nurse, as they presume that all body fluids, including wound exudate, are potentially harmful.[1]

Wound exudate can take the form of serous fluid, pus or blood-stained fluid. All three can pose a risk to the nurse if she is in contact with the exudate and it has access via cuts in her skin. The fact that HIV can be transmitted via blood means that this form of exudate has the potential to infect the nurse. Bloody exudate can be found in infected wounds and following sharp debridement. This method of debridement is not therefore recommended for patients with HIV or aquired immune deficiency syndrome (AIDS).

Patients with HIV will sustain the same wounds as the general population. Their HIV status will not prevent wound healing. During their wound history there will be the potential for viral transmission. When choosing a dressing regimen, it is worthwhile remembering that hydrocolloid dressings have the ability to contain the HIV virus *in situ* in the wound.[2] Nurses must ensure that universal precautions are adhered at all times, in order to protect themselves, their peers and their patients.

1. Kiernan M, Young T (1995) Common problems with wound care: infection with HIV. *Br J Nurs* **4**(20): 1219–23
2. Bowler PG, Delargy H, Prince D, Fondberg L (1993) The viral barrier properties of some occlusive dressings and their role in infection control. *Wounds* **5**(1): 1–8

20
Gloves should be used for all dressings

The purpose of wearing gloves for dressing changes is to protect the patient and the nurse from bacterial and viral pathogens that are transmitted via bodily fluids.[1] Previously, forceps would have been used during dressing changes. Most dressing packs now contain sterile gloves, which appear to be preferred by nurses[2]. The use of gloves, however, may lull the wearer into a false sense of security. In one study, 43% of gloves were perforated during surgical procedures.[3] Gloves are made from either latex or vinyl. Latex gloves are superior, allowing more flexibility and automatically resealing tiny punctures. Latex is, however, known to be an allergen and is therefore unsuitable for use by people who are allergic to it. Brookes' advice on good gloving practice is to choose a high quality glove, to wash hands between changing gloves and not to reuse gloves.[4]

Cuts in nurses' hands can be protected by the use of an occlusive dressing. However, this may not always be practical, eg. where there are multiple cuts in awkward places, such as between the fingers.

Bacterial contamination of the hands is best dealt with by scrupulous hand washing. Gloves may reduce compliance with this essential practice.

Certain wound dressings are extremely difficult to apply using gloves; nevertheless, strict hand hygiene is a priority in applying the dressing to prevent the nurse compromising its sterility.

1. Young T (1995) Traumatic wounds. *Practice Nurs* **6**(17): 37–40
2. Russell L (1993) Healing alternatives. *Nurs Times* **89**(42): 88–90
3. Palmer JD, Rickett JWS (1992) The mechanisms and risks of surgical glove perforation. *J Hosp Infect* **22**(4): 279–86
4. Brookes A (1994) Surgical glove perforation. *Nurs Times* **90**(21): 60–2

CHAPTER THREE
PRESSURE SORES

1

It is possible, through good nursing care, to prevent all pressure sores

It is not possible to prevent all pressure sores, but the large majority of sores are preventable. It has been estimated that while 95% of pressure damage can be avoided, the remaining 5% are inevitable.[1]

Since nurses consider the maintenance of skin integrity to be primarily their domain, they must accept some responsibility for failure to prevent tissue breakdown. The total responsibility, however, must be borne by the multidisciplinary team.

Bar and Pathy[2] assert that pressure sore formation may not be the result of lower standards of care, and that a small percentage of patients will go on to develop pressure sores despite all interventions, because of their critical state.

1. Loader S, Delve M, Hofman D (1994) A consultancy service that pays dividends. Setting up a pressure sore relief group. *Prof Nurse* **9**: 259–66
2. Bar CA, Pathy MSJ (1991) *Principles and Practice of Geriatric Medicine*. John Wiley and Sons, London

2
Pressure sores are the responsibility of the multidisciplinary team and not just the nurse

Pressure sores are a problem that concerns all health care professionals, not just the nurse. Nurses have historically considered the maintenance of skin integrity to be primarily their domain. The nurse is, however, in an ideal position to coordinate a multidisciplinary effort. The following people may be involved in this team effort:

Nurse — both hospital and community
Doctor
Clinical nurse specialist — tissue viability
Dietician
Physiotherapist
Occupational therapist
Family and carers
Social worker
Pharmacist

In addition, many more people may be involved, depending on the circumstances. No health care professional should work in isolation. Much experience and knowledge can be shared within the multidisciplinary team to provide a more satisfactory solution to the problem of pressure sores.[1]

1.   Land L (1995) A review of pressure damage prevention strategies. *J Adv Nurs* **22**: 329–37

3
Pressure sores are not only caused by pressure; shearing forces and friction are also important factors

The three external factors that cause pressure sores are pressure, shear and friction. They can occur on their own or in combination.[1]

Pressure — The skin is normally kept healthy by blood supplied through a capillary network. In some places, such as the heels, hips and sacrum, large bones lie close to the skin. When the skin is compressed between the bone and support surface as a result of pressure, that area of the skin becomes ischaemic, leading to death of the tissue and pressure sore formation.

Shear — This commonly occurs, eg. when a patient is in the sitting position, and results from the patient's sacral skin adhering to the bed linen: the deep fascia moves in a downward direction with the skeletal structure, while the sacral fascia remains attached to the sacral dermis. This results in shearing, stretching and avulsion of capillaries leading to tissue necrosis.[2]

Friction — This is caused by two surfaces moving across one another, eg. the skin and the support surface. Friction is not thought to be a primary factor in pressure sore formation, but it can exacerbate the breakdown of the epidermis. If the surfaces are moist, friction is increased.

It is also important for the nurse to consider the many internal factors leading to pressure sore formation, such as the nutritional state of the patient and body temperature.

1.   Dealey C (1994) *The Care of Wounds*. Blackwell Scientific, Oxford
2.   Collier M (1995) *Pressure Sore Development and Prevention*. Wound Care Society Education Leaflet No. 3. Wound Care Society, London

4
Research has shown that a pressure sore can develop within 24 hours

It is impossible to say exactly how long it takes for a pressure sore to develop. It is dependent on many factors which are individual to each patient. This is why it is important to assess pressure sore risk on a regular basis. If the circumstances are right, a pressure sore could develop within half an hour.

It is thought that in the majority of cases, pressure sores take several hours to develop. Carers are encouraged to reposition patients every two hours, but this may not be adequate for all patients. Spinal-injured patients are encouraged to reposition every 15 minutes.

The length of time required for a pressure sore to develop is dependent upon, for example, the magnitude of tissue deformation, the length of time that tissue deformation is applied and the intrinsic factors that make one individual more susceptible to pressure sores than another.[1]

Pressure sores that develop under the surface of the skin, nearer the bony prominence, can take up to 14 days to appear as damage to the skin.

1. Gebhardt K (1995) What causes pressure sores? *Nurs Stand* **9**(1): 48–51

5
A capillary wall will close and cause ischaemia at 32mmHg

Following the work of Landis,[1] many quote 32mmHg as the capillary closing pressure and state that pressure above this will cause tissue ischaemia and pressure sore development.

Others criticise this work for not being directed at pressure sores, for using healthy individuals as subjects and for utilizing capillaries from the skin covering a finger nail at the level of the manubrium sterni (heart level).[1]

Numerous professionals believe that there is no definitive capillary closing pressure, and that it depends on a number of factors, such as the pressure-time factor.

Some claim that internal tissue pressures are three to five times greater than surface pressure and that ischaemia can commence at as little as 8mmHg internally, which means that a safe interface pressure would be 1.6–2.6mmHg.[2]

Bar and Pathy[3] found that many authors had estimated the capillary closing pressure and that these varied from 15mmHg to 540mmHg in both human and animal studies. To date, research has not been able to establish a definitive capillary closing pressure.

1. Landis EM (1930) Microinjection studies of capillary blood pressure in human skin. *Heart* **15**: 209–28
2. Le KM, Madsen BL, Barth PW, Ksander GA, Angell JB, Vistres LM (1984) An in-depth look at pressure sores using monolithic silicone pressure sensors. *J Plast Reconstr Surg* **74**: 745–54
3. Bar CA, Pathy MSJ (1991) *Principles and Practice of Geriatric Medicine*. Wiley and Sons, London

6
Both very thin people and very fat people are at risk of developing pressure sores

An increased incidence of pressure sore development has, for some time, been noted in patients who are very thin. These patients have less subcutaneous fat to pad over their bony prominences, causing a smaller surface area and therefore a higher interface pressure. There can also be an increased risk in obese patients. Although these patients may appear to have more subcutaneous padding of their bony prominences, they also have an increased body weight, which can affect the interface pressure.

Emaciated and obese patients are also more likely to be affected by friction and shearing forces, for the same reasons as described above.

These factors place both very thin people and very fat people at higher risk of pressure sore development, but body weight is only part of the overall risk assessment of the patient.

7
It is not possible to have a pressure sore in a neonate

Children and neonates are just as likely to develop pressure sores as adults.

Neonates nursed in special care baby units are very prone to occipital pressure sore development and care must be taken to identify those neonates most at risk and take preventive measures.

Any child can be at risk of pressure sore formation following an acute illness or severe trauma.

Chronically sick or disabled children, especially those who are chair-bound, need the same assessment and preventive action as adults.

Scar tissue from healed pressure sores does not have the same strength as healthy muscle; subcutaneous fat and skin can be vulnerable for the rest of the child's life.[1] The key to successful nursing care of neonates is accurate assessment as trauma to the skin can have serious consequences.[2]

1.   Bale S, Jones V (1996) Caring for children with wounds. *J Wound Care* **5**(4): 177–80
2.   Young T (1995) Wound healing in neonates. *J Wound Care* **4**(6): 285–8

8
It is not possible to identify erythema in a coloured person

Difficulties in identifying a stage one pressure sore or non-blanching erythema in patients with darkly pigmented skin led to the setting up of a special task force in America to try to overcome the problem.[1]

Their recommendations are as follows:

- Localised skin colour changes can occur at the site of pressure. These colours differ from the patient's usual skin colour.

- The area of skin over the pressure point may appear darker than the surrounding skin.

- The area of skin over the pressure point may feel warmer to the touch, or may be taut, shiny and/or indurated. The patient may complain of pain or discomfort in the pressure areas.

The task force felt that the present definition of a stage one pressure sore, with its emphasis on redness, was not helpful in assessing dark-skinned patients, and should be changed to:

> *'For persons with darkly pigmented intact skin, assess for erythema and/or inflammation with localised changes in skin temperature in comparison to the surrounding skin, oedema and/or induration.'*

1.   Bennett MA (1995) Report of the task force on the implications for darkly pigmented intact skin in the prediction and prevention of pressure ulcers. *Adv Wound Care* **8**(6): 34–5

9
Research has shown that massaging and rubbing pressure areas increases the circulation and reduces the risk of pressure sore development

Although such massage has been used for decades it is now thought best to avoid massage over bony prominences. The scientific evidence for the use of massage to stimulate blood flow and avert pressure sore formation is not well established, whereas there is evidence to suggest that it can lead to deep tissue trauma.

During the cleansing process, care should be taken to minimise the force and friction applied to the skin.

Ek *et al*[1] found that 10 of 15 patients with skin discoloration over their bony prominences demonstrated a lower skin blood flow after massage than before massage.

Dyson[2] described a greater amount of degenerated tissue in areas exposed to massage than in non-massaged areas.

No benefit of massage on circulation can be demonstrated. However, there is evidence to suggest that it can be harmful.

1. Ek AC, Gustavsson G, Lewis DH (1985) The local skin blood flow in areas at risk for pressure sores treated with massage. *Scand J Rehabil Med* **17**(2): 81–6
2. Dyson R (1978) Bed sores — the injuries hospital staff inflict on patients. *Nurs Mirror* **146**(24): 30–32

10
Treating pressure sores with egg white and oxygen has been shown to be beneficial

This is a myth that was derived from the following facts. For many years it has been known that protein and oxygen are important in wound healing. It was therefore thought that the protein in egg white, together with topical oxygen, would aid wound healing. Egg white was applied to the wound and then dried with the piped oxygen to give a protein-rich film over the wound.

There is no evidence to support this assumption and it is a good example of ritualistic nursing practice.

Oxygen and nutrients, such as protein, are delivered to the wound in the circulation via the capillary network within the wound bed.

11
Methylated spirit/spirit pads can be a useful preventive measure in pressure sore development

Methylated and surgical spirits have been used in the past by many health care professionals.

The practice stemmed from advice given to walkers to toughen up the skin on their heels to prevent blistering. It was originally assumed that it could also help to harden the skin and prevent pressure sore damage.

The practice was in common use on orthopaedic units, where it was also used on the skin in contact with Thomas splints.

As the spirit evaporates it cools the skin and alters the temperature. There is no evidence to support the continued use of this nursing practice; it does not prevent pressure sores, but can cause many skin problems.

12
Barrier cream improves the quality of the skin to such a degree that it is less likely to develop into a pressure sore

An individual's skin may be exposed to a variety of substances that are moist: urine, faeces, perspiration, and wound exudate. Moisture can make the skin more susceptible to injury.

It is best to try to minimise skin exposure to moisture as far as possible. During the normal cleansing process, some of the skin's 'natural barrier' is lost; a mild cleansing agent should therefore be used to minimise irritation and dryness of the skin.

There is some evidence to suggest that there is an association between dry, flaky or scaling skin and an increased incidence of pressure sores. Dry skin should be treated with bland moisturisers.

When the sources of moisture cannot be controlled, a topical barrier cream may be used. Care must be taken not to massage the cream in or to cause friction in the area, as massage has been shown to have a harmful effect.

There is little research-based evidence to indicate which is the best barrier cream to use or how much effect barrier creams have on the prevention of pressure sores, although this is currently under investigation.[1]

1   Dealey C (1995) Pressure sores and incontinence: a study evaluating the use of topical agents in skin care. *J Wound Care* **4**(3): 103–5

13
Risk assessment scores can identify all patients at risk of developing pressure sores

It is claimed that risk assessment scores, such as the Norton scale, Waterlow score and Medley score,[1] provide an explicit way of assessing the risk of pressure sore development.[2]

However, studies on the accuracy of pressure sore risk scales are equivocal, and it has not been clearly demonstrated that these scales are better than clinical judgment or that they improve outcomes.[3]

The ideal risk assessment tool must demonstrate good predictive value and high sensitivity and specificity, and be easy to use. 'The sensitivity of a tool is its ability to identify the patients at risk, the specificity represents the tool's ability to identify patients who are not at risk and remain free from pressure damage.' An ideal pressure sore risk calculator would be both 100% specific and 100% sensitive, but in reality this is not possible because sensitivity and specificity have an inverse relationship: one can only be improved at the expense of the other.[5] The reliability and validity of the Medley score is currently being evaluated.[6]

1.   Williams C (1992) A comparative study of pressure sore prevention scores. *J Tiss Viability* **2**(2): 64–6
2.   Deeks JJ (1996) Pressure sore prevention: using and evaluating risk assessment tools. *Br J Nurs* **5**(5): 313–20
3.   Cullum N, Deeks J, Fletcher A *et al* (1995) The prevention and treatment of pressure sores. *Effect Health Care* **2**(1): 1–16
4.   MacDonald K (1995) The reliability of pressure sore risk assessment tools. *Prof Nurse* **11**(3): 169–72
5.   Flanagan M (1995) Who is at risk of a pressure sore: A practical review of risk assessment systems. *Prof Nurse* **10**(5): 305–8
6.   Williams C, Fonseca J (1993) Evaluation of the Medley Score. Part one: the study plan. *Proceedings of the Third European Conference on Advances in Wound Management*, 19–22 October. Macmillan, London: 128–9

14
All patients at risk of developing pressure sores must be repositioned every two hours

Time-honoured prophylaxis for pressure sores has been frequent change in posture, day and night. Empirically, two-hourly turns have been found to be effective in the majority of patients.[1] Healthy subjects change their position much more frequently and rarely remain in any one position for two hours.

A useful technique for detecting pressure damage is to apply light finger-tip pressure to a reddened area. If the area blanches (becomes white) and then returns to the reddened colour the circulation is intact (blanching erythema). If the skin remains red on application of finger-tip pressure, the erythema is said to be non-blanching, indicating pressure damage.

Pressure relief can be achieved by manual repositioning of patients, but the following need to be taken into account when deciding on the frequency:

- The risk status of the patient — taking into consideration the intrinsic and extrinsic factors using a validated risk assessment score

- The type of support system the patient is lying or sitting on, eg. whether it is a static or a dynamic system

For example, a very high risk patient being nursed on a dynamic alternating-pressure mattress may be effectively having his/her position changed every 2.5–3 minutes. A manual change in position in this case may be performed for social reasons, such as a change of view or at mealtimes and during visiting. Frequent checking of the skin for signs of redness and heat over pressure areas would need to be undertaken to determine how long a patient can be left in one position. This will depend on what type of support surface he/she is lying on.

1.   Bar CA, Pathy MSJ (1991) *Principles and Practice of Geriatric Medicine*. John Wiley and Sons, London: 1037–60

15
All patients who are identified as being at risk of developing pressure sores should have access to a special pressure-relieving mattress

Not all patients who are identified as being at risk of developing pressure sores need a high-tech preventive mattress.[1,2] It depends very much on the risk status and general condition of the patient.

Patients with a low to moderate risk may usually be managed successfully by frequent manual repositioning and good skin care. They may be nursed on a good quality foam mattress and/or a pressure-relieving cushion.

Patients at high risk of developing pressure sores, however, need to be managed on an alternating-pressure mattress or low air loss system.

It is important that the risk assessment system incorporates a guide to equipment selection to help the health care worker choose an appropriate support system for the individual patient.

Over-allocation of expensive equipment is just as costly as under-allocation and subsequent pressure sore development.

1.   Williams C (1995) Nimbus and Alpha X Cell. *Br J Nurs* **4**(6): 351–4
2.   Lowthian P (1995) Pegasus Airwave and Bi-wave Plus. *Br J Nurs* **4**(17): 1020–4

16
Only patients using wheelchairs require a pressure-relieving cushion

It is not only patients in wheelchairs who may need pressure-relieving cushions; the many patients who sit in ordinary chairs may also benefit from their use.

Lowry[1] claims that often only superficial attention is paid to seating, and suggests that nurses, especially those concerned with wound care, should demand adequate provision for their patients. Many manufacturers have developed special seating and pressure-relieving cushions for both wheelchairs and ordinary chairs. These are available in all shapes and sizes to suit any situation. Many hospital patients sit for long periods in 'day room' type chairs, and pressure relief must be considered depending on the risk status of the patient.

There are also many cushions available for the very high risk patients, to complement the alternating-pressure mattress on which they may be nursed.

1. Lowry M (1992) Hospital seating and pressure areas. *Nurs Stand* **6**(3): 10–11

17
Research has proved that sitting a patient on a rubber or air-filled ring can cause more damage and does not help to prevent pressure sores

Rubber or air-filled rings are known to cause venous congestion and oedema, but the strength of the evidence is not well documented.

Crewe[1], in a study of at-risk patients, found that ring cushions were more likely to cause pressure sores than prevent them.

As early as 1930, researchers had expressed doubts about the wisdom of using ring cushions. Subsequent research has shown that lymphatic drainage and blood circulation are adversely affected by the pressure produced. This damage can lead to pressure sore development.[2,3]

The use of ring cushions must be questioned and ritualistic practice replaced by research-based practice.

Lowthian[4] calls for the abolition of the ring cushion as it is positively harmful.

1.   Crewe RA (1987) Problems of rubber ring nursing cushions and a clinical survey of alternative cushions for ill patients. *Care Sci Pract* **5**(2): 9–11
2.   Deacon L (1986) Pressure sores — does anyone read re- search? *Nurs Times* **83**(32): 57–9
3.   Kennedy J (1989) Ring cushions — an outmoded treatment. *Nurs Times* **85**(48): 34–5
4.   Lowthian P (1985) A sore point. *Nurs Times* **161**(9): 30–32

18
Sheepskins are an effective pressure sore preventing support surface

There are two types of sheepskins: 100% wool and 100% polyester.

Both products have been evaluated by the Department of Health[1], which has concluded that these products do not provide any pressure relief and should only be used as comfort aids.

When new and in good condition these products can reduce some of the friction and help to prevent sweating, but their condition soon deteriorates, especially after laundering.

They should only be used for patients with a low risk of developing pressure sores.

1. Medical Devices Agency (1994) *Evaluation of Static Mattress Overlays*. Department of Health, London

19
A latex glove filled with water and placed under a heel can be useful in preventing heel pressure sores

The use of water-filled gloves for pressure relief on heels has been described as ritualistic, outdated nursing practice.[1]

Research has indicated that the practice has little or no beneficial effect[2], and that in some cases it could be detrimental, causing increased pressure under the heel.[3]

Lockyer-Stevens[2] demonstrated, in his pilot study, that pressure relief when using water-filled gloves under the heel did not reach the 'accepted' threshold of 32mmHg, and did not prevent tissue ischaemia and a resulting pressure sore. Three volunteers of varying weights were selected and three gloves of different sizes filled with varying amounts of water were tested. Lockyer-Stevens noted that water-filled gloves tended to be applied haphazardly, with no effort made to apply the correct therapeutic pressure, and that they were regularly used in intensive care, vascular surgery, trauma and orthopaedic units.

Williams[3] found that in a sample of 40 (20 healthy volunteers and 20 patients) the pressure on the heel was increased by an average of 12.5% when using the water-filled glove. In this study, gloves were filled with 260ml of water, which was found to be the average amount used in clinical practice. The hand-held Talley skin pressure evaluator was used to measure interface pressure, although the accuracy of this instrument is known to be limited.

The use of water-filled gloves is a popular, yet clearly ineffective, method of preventing pressure sores on the heel. In order to be accountable, nurses must take responsibility for their actions and base their care on valid clinical research.[4]

1.   Anon (1993) Using water-filled gloves for pressure relief. *J Wound Care* **2**(3): 136
2.   Lockyer-Stevens N (1993) The use of water-filled gloves to prevent the formation of decubitus ulcers on the heel. *J Wound Care* **2**(5): 282–5
3.   Williams C (1993) Using water-filled gloves for pressure relief on heels. *J Wound Care* **2**(6): 345–8
4.   United Kingdom Central Council for Nursing, Midwifery and Health Visiting (1992) *Code of Professional Conduct for the Nurse, Midwife and Health Visitor.* UKCC, London

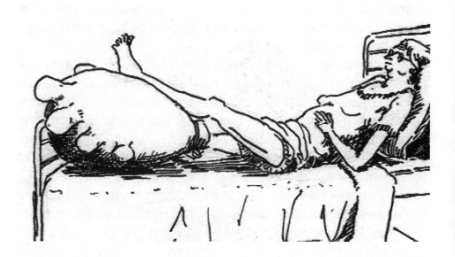

20
Measuring interface pressure is the only way of evaluating the effectiveness of a support surface

Measuring interface pressure is one of several ways of evaluating the effectiveness of a support surface, and there is much debate between the experts as to which method is most useful. Pressure measurements at the interface of the skin and the support surface have been widely employed by investigators for comparing various beds and mattresses.[1] Many devices are available for measuring pressure interface: thinner and smaller transducers have been found to be more reliable.

Measurement of skin temperature by means of thermography is another method of evaluating the effectiveness of a support surface. There is a positive relationship between local blood flow and skin temperature. A rise in temperature of 1°C can increase oxygen demand and metabolic activity by 10%.[1] Changes in skin temperature are a valuable guide to the condition of the skin. The measurement of skin temperature is influenced by factors, such as air convection, heat radiation from lights or other sources.

Assessment of skin oxygen tension is another method. In this method, skin tissue perfusion and oxygenation are measured by means of a transcutaneous sensor.

Low pressure for long periods has a more damaging affect on the skin than high pressure sustained over short periods. 'An inverse relationship between the intensity and the duration of pressure, to produce tissue damage,' has been demonstrated.[1] It is suggested that pressure impulse representing the area under the pressure-time curve should be used for comparisons of support surfaces.[2]

1. Rithalia SVS (1991) Pressure sores: methods used for the assessment of patient support surfaces. *Clin Rehabil* **5**: 323–9
2. Bennett L, Lee BY (1988) Vertical shear existence in animal pressure threshold experiments. *Decubitus* **1**: 18–24

CHAPTER
LEG ULCERS

eg ulcer is a diagnosis

It is unacceptable to offer leg ulcer as a diagnosis. The ulcer is not the disease, but a manifestation of the underlying disease process.[1] The underlying disease process must be identified as soon as possible by a thorough holistic assessment.

The principal causes of leg ulcers are venous disease, arterial disease, or a combination of the two. Other more unusual causes include neuropathy, vasculitis, malignancy, infection, blood disorders, metabolic disease and trauma.

Over 70% of leg ulcers occur as a result of venous disease, 10% as a result of arterial disease and 10–15% as a result of combined arterial and venous disease. The more unusual causes account for 2–5% of leg ulcers.

Chronic venous hypertension is usually due to incompetent veins. Arterial disease could be due to atherosclerotic occlusion of large vessels, leading to tissue ischaemia.[2]

1.   Young T (1994) Treatment of mixed aetiology leg ulcers. *Br J Nurs* **3**(12): 598–601
2.   Morison MJ, Moffatt C (1994) *A Colour Guide to the Assessment and Management of Leg Ulcers*. Mosby – Times International Publishers, New York: 10

2
You normally have a leg ulcer for life

It has been thought for generations that once you have a leg ulcer you have it for life. This belief persists because, until recently, many people suffered from leg ulcers for 20–30 years.

This view of leg ulcers normally relates to venous leg ulcers which come and go over many years.

It is true to say that once you have venous disease you have it for life, but once you have an active, effective treatment regimen, beginning with compression bandaging and then compression hosiery, there is no need, in the majority of cases, for venous leg ulcers to continue for years on end.

Major developments in technology have also improved the healing rates for arterial and diabetic leg ulcers.

There will always be some patients with leg ulcers that do not heal despite all attempts at treatment and the use of research-based care. These patients need to be fully investigated so that a better understanding is gained into their disease process.

3
Men and women are equally likely to suffer from a leg ulcer

Men and women under 40 years of age have a similar prevalence of leg ulceration, but with increasing age the prevalence in women is higher.

Overall the ratio of females to males affected by leg ulceration is approximately 2:1. Some say it is a condition of older females. The cause of the female predominance is unclear, but it is thought to be related to pregnancy, frequent childbirth and venous thrombosis. More recently, a rise in the proportion of males affected has been noted. This is thought to be a side-effect of the increase in male longevity.

There appears to be considerable variation in the reported male to female ratios, some of which can be explained by discrepancies in study design.

The weight of evidence suggests that ulceration is more common in women and it would seem that female predominance is age-related and particularly marked in later life.

4

Patients with leg ulcers should not have a shower or bath in case their ulcer gets wet

It is acceptable practice for patients with leg ulcers to cleanse these in warm tap water and such patients can therefore have a bath or a shower. To date there is no published work to support this practice in leg ulcer care. However, a randomised study has been carried out in Sweden comparing the infection and healing rates in 705 patients with acute traumatic soft tissue wounds that were cleansed with either tap water or sterile saline. The authors found no detrimental effects from the tap water and recommended that it should be the cleansing solution of choice.[1] Cullum and Roe[2] state that 'there is no evidence that complete immersion of the leg in warm water does any harm; indeed, it may be psychologically beneficial for patients to have their limbs bathed and may also improve local circulation and benefit the skin'.

Two factors that may influence this practice are the quality of local tap water and the alternative methods available. If bottles of sterile water/saline are used (a common practice if the area to be cleansed is large) then the nurse must be aware of the potential for bacterial contamination of the solution once the bottle is opened.[3]

Many practitioners use a large bucket lined with a waterproof plastic liner to hold the cleansing solution, enabling the patient to immerse the entire lower leg in the solution. This allows patients to bathe their legs effectively and has a positive effect on patient well-being. The liner can then be disposed of in the waste system, eliminating the possibility of cross-infection, and making the system reusable.[4]

It is now well established that all chronic wounds contain large numbers of bacteria, and these do not normally delay healing. It is only a clinical systemic infection that may delay wound healing. It is therefore unnecessary to use an aseptic technique to cleanse these wounds, as there is no need to completely remove the bacteria.

The indication that tap water may be a satisfactory cleansing agent has been confirmed, and tap water is now used for cleansing wounds by leaders in the field.[5]

1. Angeras MH, Brondberg A, Falk A, Seaman T (1992) Comparison between sterile saline and tap water for the cleansing of acute traumatic soft tissue wounds. *Eur J Surg* **158**: 347–50
2. Cullum N, Roe B (1995) *Leg Ulcers: Nursing Management: A Research-Based Guide*. Scutari Press, Harrow
3. Brown DG, Skyliss TP, Sulisz CA, Friedman C, Richter DR (1985) Sterile water and saline solution: potential reservoirs of nosocomial infection. *Am J Infect Control* **13**(1): 35–9
4. Gilchrist B (1994) Treating bacterial wound infection *Nurs Times* **90**(50): 55–8
5. Young T (1995) Common problems in wound care: wound cleansing. *Br J Nurs* **4**(5): 286–9

5
The best health care setting in which to treat leg ulcer patients is the hospital

The best health care setting is one that is closest to the patient's normal environment, ie. at home in the community. It is pointless bringing a patient into hospital without considering the social circumstances and the environment into which the patient will be discharged. It should be noted, however, that many homes cannot be described as a good health care setting.

The treatment of leg ulceration has historically been delegated predominantly to district nurses. Nationally, district nurses spend up to half their time treating leg ulcers. Until recently, treatment has been based on marketing pressures and not on research-based evidence.

Many now believe that community-based clinics offer an effective means of achieving healing in many leg ulcer patients.[1] Where necessary, patients may be referred to hospital-based professionals, such as a vascular surgeon or dermatologist, from the community-based clinics.

Community leg ulcer clinics have been established in a number of areas in this country. They have been shown to use community nurse time effectively.

Improved healing is largely dependent on the use of effective research-based regimens.[2]

1. Moffatt CJ, Franks PJ, Oldroyd M *et al* (1992) Community clinics for leg ulcers and impact on healing. *Br Med J* **305**: 1389–92
2. Cullum N, Roe B (1995) The organisation and delivery of leg ulcer care. In: *Leg Ulcers: Nursing Management: A Research-Based Guide*. Scutari Press, Harrow: 135–48

6
When undertaking a Doppler assessment it is only necessary to record the ankle/brachial pressure index (ABPI) in the arm and leg on the ulcerated side. The only foot pulse to use is the dorsalis pedis

The ABPI is a comparison of the highest ankle pressure and the best estimate of central systolic blood pressure. The latter measurement is taken to be the highest of the two (left and right) brachial pressures.[1] The brachial pressure can vary between left and right arms, even in healthy subjects.

The highest occlusion pressure for the ankle pulses, including the posterior tibial and dorsalis pedis, should be taken as the best estimate of the ankle systolic pressure.

A review of the recent literature on this topic and a guide to calculating the ABPI is given by Vowden *et al.*[1] It recommends assessment of brachial pressures in both arms, and foot pulses in both legs.

1.   Vowden KR, Goulding V, Vowden P (1996) Hand-held Doppler assessment for peripheral arterial disease. *J Wound Care* **5**(3): 125–8

7

The only gel that should be used when performing a Doppler assessment is ultrasound transmission gel

Ultrasound is the term used to describe very high frequency sounds which are outside the normal hearing range.[1]

A Doppler signal is obtained with an angle of about 45° between the transducer and the artery. It is important to use liberal amounts of conducting ultrasound transmission gel between the transducer and the body to obtain good results since air is a poor transmitter of sound. Ultrasound transmission gel is specially designed to transmit sound and is therefore the only gel that should be used for this purpose.

Gels that are not designed for use with ultrasound may give a poor sound quality and false readings. They also become too liquid at body temperature. A gel in popular use is lubricating gel, but this is not designed for use with ultrasound and therefore should not be used for this purpose.

1. Williams C (1995) HNE diagnostics Dopplex ultrasound machines. *Br J Nurs* **4**(22): 1340–44

8
Only venous leg ulcers occur in the gaiter area

Venous leg ulcers frequently occur in the gaiter area (between the malleolus and mid-calf), usually near the medial malleolus and sometimes near the lateral malleolus, but can occur anywhere on the leg.[1]

Arterial leg ulcers usually occur on the foot or lateral aspect of the leg, but again may occur anywhere on the limb, including near the medial malleolus, which is a common site for a venous leg ulcer.

The skin overlying the tibia is poorly vascularised and is a common site for vasculitic ulcers and pretibial laceration resulting from trauma.[1]

The site and appearance of the ulcer is only one aspect of the overall assessment of the patient with a leg ulcer, and therefore diagnosis should not be made on this one aspect alone.

1.   Negus D (1995) *Leg Ulcers: A Practical Approach to Management* 2nd edn. Butterworth-Heinemann, Oxford

9
Venous leg ulcers are not painful

It is commonly believed that many patients with venous leg ulcers do not experience pain. However, it is now known that they do suffer from pain, but that the pain is very different from that experienced by patients with arterial leg ulcers.

Through quality of life studies we can investigate patients' perceptions of their leg ulcers and the impact of a leg ulcer on their well-being and lifestyle. Hofman *et al*[1] conclude from their study of 140 patients, that venous ulcers are painful and that the pain is in three distinct locations; within the ulcer, around the ulcer and elsewhere in the leg. They state that the presence of severe pain does not necessarily indicate arterial disease or infection, and that pain is, in general, inadequately controlled in these patients.

Venous leg ulcer pain is normally described as a constant dull ache or pain.

There are two types of arterial leg ulcer pain. Claudication is described as a sharp cramp-like pain in the muscles of the leg, which is usually relieved by resting or hanging the leg over the bed or sleeping upright in a chair. Rest pain occurs in patients with critical leg ischaemia and is severe and persistent.[2]

1.	Hofman D, Ryan TJ, Arnold F *et al* (1997) Pain in venous leg ulcers. *J Wound Care* **6**(5): 222–4
2.	*Second European Consensus Document on Chronic Critical Leg Ischaemia* (1991) Supplement to *Circulation* **84**(4): 1–26

10
Varicose eczema is caused by a sensitivity reaction to dressings

This is a myth. Although people think that varicose eczema is caused by a sensitivity reaction to dressings, this is not the case. Varicose eczema, also known as stasis eczema, is associated with venous insufficiency. Varicose eczema can also be a complication of chronic venous hypertension. It is not caused by a sensitivity reaction to dressings, but can be aggravated by a number of wound care products, through irritation and allergy.[1]

Sensitisation to wound care products may result in contact dermatitis, which is commonly seen in leg ulcer patients.[2] The most common causes of sensitivity reactions are topical antibiotics and the bases and preservatives used in ointments.[3]

Treatment options include topical steroids and paste bandages. Occasionally, however, some of the constituents of these treatments may aggravate the condition.

1   Cameron J (1995) Contact sensitivity and eczema in leg ulcer patients. In: *Leg Ulcers: Nursing Management: A Research-Based Guide*. Scutari Press, Harrow: 101–12

2. Wilson CL, Cameron J, Powell SM, Cherry G, Ryan TJ (1991) High incidence of contact dermatitis in leg ulcer patients — implications for management. *Clin Exp Dermatol* **16**: 250–3

3. Bahmer FA (1989) Local factors that might promote the development of contact allergies in patients with chronic venous insufficiency. In: Davy A, Stemmer R, eds. *Phebologie*. Libbey, London: 110–12

11
The best form of compression bandaging is the Charing Cross four-layer bandage

There are three types of compression bandage: short stretch, long stretch and multi-layer. The Charing Cross four-layer bandage is a multi-layer bandage.

Much research into the three groups has been undertaken and all have demonstrated good healing rates with venous leg ulcers. There is no concrete evidence that any one group of bandages is much better than another.

The different types, however, have different advantages and these should be considered on an individual basis when deciding upon a compression bandage.

Short-stretch bandages are very popular in European countries and are said to be very comfortable for the patient. They are also considered to be more useful for ambulant patients, particularly when ischaemia is suspected. The active calf muscle provides the pressure required. This type of bandage is therefore not suitable for inactive individuals.[1]

Long-stretch bandages have the advantage that there are three different types of bandage in this group available to the community nurse on Drug Tariff. This type of bandage is also less bulky than some of the other compression bandages. Long-stretch bandages are a cost-effective option as they can be washed and reused. One disadvantage is that high pressures may result if the bandage is inexpertly applied.

The multi-layer bandage can stay in place and maintain good pressures for up to seven days.[2] It is therefore considered to be a safer option as it is a combination of bandages producing the pressure. It is also less likely to give very high pressure readings if applied incorrectly.[3]

Each patient needs to be assessed on an individual basis before a compression bandage is selected. The lifestyle and care setting are important factors in the decision.

1. Thomas S (1996) High compression bandages. *J Wound Care* **5**(1): 40–3
2. Williams C (1995) Coban. *Br J Nurs* **4**(3): 172–4
3. Morison M, Moffatt C (1994) *A Colour Guide to the Assessment and Management of Leg Ulcers*. 2nd edn. Mosby, London

12
Circular and figure-of-eight bandaging techniques result in different levels of compression

A major factor in the level of compression achieved with compression bandaging is operator technique. In clinical practice, medical and nursing staff apply a compression bandage at the tension that they consider appropriate. The level of pressure required to treat venous leg disease has not yet been agreed upon internationally.[1]

Judgement as to the level of pressure required is subjective and major differences will occur between the pressures achieved by different individuals.

Barbenel *et al*[2] demonstrated that bandages applied in a figure-of-eight configuration resulted in pressures that were approximately 1.5–2 times greater than those produced when the same bandages were applied in the form of a spiral with a 50% overlap.

1. Nelson EA (1995) Compression therapy for leg disorders. *J Wound Care* **5**(4): 162–4
2. Barbenel JC, Sockalingham S, Queen D (1990) *In vivo* and laboratory evaluation of elastic bandages. *Care Sci Pract* **8**: 72–4

13
When a venous leg ulcer has healed, the compression can be discontinued

It has now been established that compression therapy is the treatment of choice for patients with venous leg ulcers. Healing has been shown to take place in a matter of months for the majority of patients when the treatment is applied correctly.

Compression bandaging improves the function of the calf muscle pump and reduces venous hypertension, which in turn leads to healing.[1] If compression bandaging were to be discontinued following healing then the venous hypertension would return and the leg ulcer would recur.

Recurrence of leg ulcers is very common[2], and it is vital that patients and health care professionals understand that compression therapy must continue for the rest of the patient's life to prevent the leg ulcer recurring. This can take the form of compression hosiery and can be very acceptable to both male or female patients. The exact amount of pressure needed to prevent recurrence is not known, although it is know to be dependent on the severity of the venous disease. Accordingly, a class 2–3 stocking is normally used. Correct fitting is of vital importance. Graduated compression hosiery is regarded as an essential component of prevention of ulcer recurrence. Research supporting its use is sparse. However, medical and nursing clinicians recognise its value in clinical practice.[3]

Surgical intervention may also contribute to preventing recurrence by addressing the underlying cause.

Education and support are needed by the patient with a healed ulcer, and clinics and support groups have been shown to keep recurrence at minimal levels.[4]

1.   Williams C (1996) Treatment of venous leg ulcers: 2. *Br J Nurs* **5**(5): 274–82
2.   Callam˙MJ, Ruckley CV, Harper DR , Dale JJ (1985) Chronic ulceration of the leg: extent of the problem and provision of care. *Br Med J* **290**: 1855–6
3.   Moffatt CJ, Dorman MC (1995) Recurrence of leg ulcers within a community ulcer service. *J Wound Care* **4**(9): 57–61
4.   Ruane-Morris M, Thompson G, Lawton S (1995) Supporting patients with healed leg ulcers. *Prof Nurse* **10**(12): 765–70

14
If a leg ulcer has a mixed aetiology it is not possible to use compression therapy

The treatment of mixed aetiology leg ulcers is very much dependent on the overall assessment and ankle/brachial pressure index (ABPI).

When the ABPI is below 0.5 the patient will require referral to a vascular surgeon. When the APBI is above 0.8 it is possible to use compression bandaging.

For patients with an APBI between 0.7 and 0.8 it may be possible to use a reduced or light form of compression with more frequent follow-up. Leg ulcer patients with an ABPI of less than 0.7 may benefit from referral for a full vascular assessment by a vascular team.

General advice on rest/exercise, position/elevation, footwear, environment and skin care can also help to protect the limb.[1]

ABPI<0.5	Refer to vascular surgeon: **urgent**
ABPI 0.5–0.7	Refer to vascular surgeon: non-urgent
ABPI 0.7–0.8	Light compression or refer for vascular assessment
ABPI >0.8	Compression bandaging

1. Young T (1994) Treatment of mixed aetiology leg ulcers. *Br J Nurs* **3**(12): 598–601

15
Arterial ulcers always result in gangrene and amputation

Arterial leg ulcers do not always result in gangrene and amputation. The outcome usually depends on the cause.

The underlying pathology will include some degree of arterial involvement in 25–30% of all patients with leg ulcers.[1]

The most common cause of reduced blood flow is atherosclerosis, a build-up of plaque in the lumen of the artery.

A less common cause is an embolus. If not removed quickly an embolus can result in persistent ischaemia.[1]

The management of arterial ulcers must include a thorough assessment, including medical history and identification of risk factors such as smoking and hypertension.[2]

A vascular assessment is also required. This can be performed using a hand-held Doppler and calculating the ankle/brachial pressure index. This can give an estimate of the degree of arterial insufficiency.

In patients who are suitable for surgery, arterial bypass may improve the blood supply. Those who are unfit for surgery may benefit from angioplasty. Management also includes pain control, infection control, dressings, non-restrictive bandaging and education.

1. Cameron J (1996) Arterial leg ulcers. *Nurs Stand* **10**(26): 50–53
2. Vowden KR, Vowden P (1996) Arterial disease: reversible and irreversible risk factors. *J Wound Care* **5**(2): 89–90

16

A Doppler ultrasound machine is only able to assess a patient's arterial blood supply

This is not the case. A hand-held Doppler can be used for three purposes:

1.	to assess arterial blood supply
2.	to assess venous blood supply
3.	to assess fetal blood supply

Doppler assessment of the arterial supply is the most common assessment performed by health care professionals who deal with leg ulcer patients. It is normally performed to enable calculation of the ankle/brachial pressure index to determine whether the ulcer is a venous or arterial leg ulcer, and, if it is a venous leg ulcer, whether compression therapy is indicated.

Doppler ultrasound is a quick and painless investigation, which patients prefer.[1]

Doppler ultrasound can also be very effective in assessment of the venous system of the leg. The competence of venous valves can be demonstrated and thrombosis can be detected. For venous valve incompetence the patient is assessed in a standing position.

A hand-held Doppler may help the practitioner to obtain a great deal of useful information about the extent of disease in the vascular system.[1]

1. Stubbing N (1996) Using non-invasive methods to perform vascular assessment. *Nurs Stand* **10**(45): 49–50

17
Diabetic ulcers are caused by peripheral vascular disease

Ulceration of the lower limb, especially the foot, is a common complication of diabetes mellitus. In this condition, ulcers may be caused by peripheral vascular disease, by peripheral neuropathy, or by a combination of the two.

Neuropathy is the commonest complication of diabetes and may cause loss of sensation or paraesthesia in the feet.[1] It can also cause deformities of the foot and gait. Prolonged pressure will lead to ulceration.

Peripheral vascular disease may not be the initial cause of ulcer development, but it makes healing the ulcer much more difficult.

Diabetic ulcers are often graded according to the Wagner classification of foot ulceration[2]:

Grade 0	No lesion
Grade 1	Superficial skin loss
Grade 2	Deeper lesion
Grade 3	Abscess or osteomyelitis
Grade 4	Partial gangrene
Grade 5	Extensive gangrene

Care of the diabetic patient with foot problems requires the skill of a team of health care professionals. Without full integration of and communication between team members, there is considerable scope for problems to arise.[3]

1. Barnett A (1992) Prevention and treatment of the diabetic foot ulcer. *Br J Nurs* **2**(1): 7–10
2. Wagner FW (1983) Algorithms of diabetic foot care. In: Levin ME, O'Neal FW, eds. *The Diabetic Foot*. CV Mosby, St Louis
3. Young M (1993) *Blueprint for the Management of Diabetic Foot Ulceration*. ConvaTec, Uxbridge

18
You only see malignancy in fungating wounds, not in leg ulcers

Although malignant ulcers are rare, it is possible for a leg ulcer to become malignant or a skin tumour to become ulcerated.

Malignancy can be identified and confirmed by biopsy. Malignancy should be an early consideration if the ulcer has an unusual appearance, or fails to heal despite every effort.

When a squamous cell carcinoma develops in a chronic venous leg ulcer it is known as a Marjolin's ulcer.

Signs to look out for are a rolled edge, any overgrowth of tissue in the base of the wound or at its margins, or a dark-red unhealthy wound bed.

19
Vasculitic ulcers only occur in patients with rheumatoid arthritis

Vasculitic ulcers are normally associated with rheumatoid arthritis, but can occur in other, less common, inflammatory connective tissue disorders. The ulcers are small, painful and often multiple. They are seen in patients with polyarteritis nodosa and systemic lupus erythematosus. Vasculitic ulcers are often slow to heal and affected by the underlying disease.

It has been reported that up to 10% of people with rheumatoid arthritis develop a leg ulcer at some stage. The reason why these patients develop leg ulcers is not completely understood, but it is thought to be a combination of vasculitis (inflammation of the blood vessels), poor venous return and the effects of prolonged steroid therapy on the skin.

20
You can get a leg ulcer as a result of having an inflammatory bowel disease

There is a type of leg ulcer called pyoderma gangrenosum which occurs in people with an associated chronic inflammatory disease such as ulcerative colitis and Chrohn's disease, and also in patients with leukaemia and polyarthritis.[1]

The ulcer can occur anywhere on the body but is most common on the leg. Because it is often misdiagnosed it is often mismanaged.

The lesion often starts as a pustule or as a red inflamed nodule with a violet border that can rapidly develop into an ulcer.

This condition is not bacterial in origin, but its pathogenesis, which is presumably immunological, is not fully understood.

Pyoderma gangrenosum is diagnosed clinically as the pathology is non-specific.[2] The condition responds to systemic steroids but not antibiotics.

1.   Samuel J, Williams C (1996) Pyoderma gangrenosum: an inflammatory ulcer. *J Wound Care* **5**(7): 314–18
2:   Mitchell Sams Jr. W (1990) Inflammatory ulcers: pyoderma gangrenosum. In: Mitchell Sams Jr. W, Lynch PJ (eds). *Principles and Practice of Dermatology*. Churchill Livingstone, London: 901–5

Myth and reality in wound care

CHAPTER FIVE
WOUND MANAGEMENT

1
A dressing is a medical device

If it were only that simple!

A dressing may be categorised as either a medical device or a medicinal product.

Dressings that are classified as medicinal products are governed by the Medicines Control Agency, which is under the jurisdiction of the Medicines Act 1968. Such dressings carry a product licence because they make a specific medicinal claim about their action. Within the Medicines Act there are three classes of medicinal products:

1. **General sale list medicines** — these can be bought over the counter from outlets without the supervision of a pharmacist, eg. certain iodine-based products

2. **Pharmacy medicines** — these can be bought over the counter in registered pharmaceutical establishments, eg. paste bandages

3. **Prescription-only medicines** — these can only be obtained from a pharmacist on receipt of a prescription, eg. topical antibiotic preparations

Dressings that are medicated therefore come under the Medicines Act, and dressings that do not achieve their principal intended outcome by pharmacological means are classified as medical devices.[1]

The Medical Device Directorate is part of the Department of Health. It is responsible for the safety, quality and effectiveness of all medical devices used in the National Health Service and other health care sectors. Dressings that are classified as medical devices are governed by the 1995 Medical Device Directive. The dressing has to achieve its intended claimed performance and be fit and safe for that purpose. If certain criteria are fulfilled then the dressing is issued with a CE mark;

possession of a CE mark will be mandatory for classification as a medical device by June 1998. Medical devices are split into four groups depending on their level of perceived risk to the patient. Devices that fall into the higher risk categories, eg. classes two and three, have to be backed by clinical research studies before they can be marketed. Most wound dressing products fall into these categories and the CE mark is visible on their packaging.

The issue of what is a device and what is a medicine is not always clear. Some dressing products fall between the two definitions and each product should be checked for its individual status.

1.   Kurring PA (1996) An Introduction to Wound Management and the Clinical Investigation of Wound Management Devices in the UK and Europe. Thesis. University of Wales, Cardiff

2
If a dressing has not worked in three days then it needs to be changed to another product

Before any wound treatment can be initiated, a holistic assessment must be undertaken. This should include the clinical appearance of the wound. The nurse must decide whether the wound contains necrotic or sloughy tissue, whether it is clinically infected, and whether it is granulating or epithelialising.[1] This part of the assessment will mainly indicate what dressing should be used.

If the nurse is confident in his/her assessment, the treatment should only be changed when the clinical appearance changes. For example, a hydrogel may be used initially to deslough a wound. When this has been achieved and the wound is granulating, the dressing may need to be changed to a hydrocolloid.

The only other reason for changing a treatment regimen is that, for some reason, the patient is not happy with it or it is not suitable.

It is important to remember that it is not the dressing that heals the wound. The dressing only promotes the ideal healing environment. If the underlying cause of the wound is not identified then healing may not take place, and it is not the fault of the dressing but the assessment.

1.   Collier M (1994) Assessing a wound. *Nurs Stand* **8**(49): 3–8

3
Dressings can be used in combination to make a more efficient product

All health care professionals are accountable for their actions and must take great care when using a combination of dressings.

Some dressings made by the same company are designed to be used together, eg. a hydrocolloid paste and hydrocolloid wafer for a cavity wound, or a hydrocolloid gel and a hydrocolloid wafer for a sloughy or necrotic wound. In these situations the company has clinical evidence that these dressings are safe and effective to use in combination and the evidence is documented within their directions for use.

No dressings should be used together unless it is specified within the directions for use accompanying the product, or you have written documentation from the companies involved, that it is safe to do so.

A common combination is a hydrogel and an alginate. In this situation there can be no rationale for this treatment regimen as one product is designed to absorb exudate from highly exuding wounds, and the other to rehydrate a dry wound and encourage the removal of slough and necrotic tissue.

To be safe, always check with the companies involved and ensure that there is a good rationale for the chosen combination.

4
District nurses do not have access to the same range of dressings as hospital nurses

This is a reality. There is restricted access to dressings for district nurses because of the *Drug Tariff*. The *Drug Tariff* is a book that contains details of all drugs, dressings and appliances that a GP can prescribe. Like the *British National Formulary*, it is updated monthly and distributed to GPs and community pharmacists. It is compiled by the Prescription Pricing Authority for the Department of Health. Dressings that are specified as prescribable by Gps in the Tariff may be supplied to patients in the community on FP10 (GP10 in Scotland).[1] If the GP prescribes a dressing that is not in the Tariff and the pharmacist dispenses it, then he/she cannot be reimbursed for the prescription by the Department of Health. In essence, they would be supplying the dressing free of charge!

On first inspection the range of wound dressings available would appear to be comprehensive. On closer examination, however, cavity and deodorising dressings are seen to be absent. Consequently the range of dressings does not reflect the needs of the patient population in the community setting. This is a very frustrating situation for district nurses. To obtain a non-Tariff dressing, it has been known for a GP to prescribe a dressing that is in the Tariff and of a similar price to the one that is not in the Tariff. The pharmacist then dispenses the one that is not in the Tariff but claims back the money for the one that is in the Tariff. This is commonly referred to a 'doing a swop'. The practice is illegal and the patient is receiving a dressing that is different from the one that was prescribed. This subterfuge, only hides the problem, and it would be better to lobby for changes to the existing practice of only allowing a Tariff dressing to be prescribed.

In the current climate of collaborative care, hospitals who discharge patients using a dressing that is not in the Tariff will often continue to supply the dressing to ensure continuity of care. However, this practice may become the victim of financial restraint.

The problem of access to dressings may be reversed, with hospital nurses becoming the victims, if, usually for financial reasons, the hospital formulates a dressings policy that restricts the range of dressings available to hospital staff.

The solution therefore must be for hospital and community staff to be aware of the restrictions imposed upon each other; unfortunately, as shown in the literature, this is not always the case.[2,3]

If a mutual understanding is established then hopefully the victim of the restrictions will no longer be the patients and their wounds.

1. Dale J (1995) Wound dressings on the drug tariff. *Prof Nurse* **10**(7): 461–5
2. Phillips S, Frost J (1993) A barrier to the continuity of care. *Prof Nurse* **8**(8): 536–42
3. Young T (1994) Wound management: the hospital—community divide. *Br J Nurs* **3**(14): 702–6

5
Hospital and community staff pay the same price for their dressing products

There are two main supply routes for wound dressing products in existence: one to hospitals and one to the community.

The hospital route is influenced by The National Health Service Supplies Authority (NHSSA), which has in the past consisted of a number of supplies divisions, each with its own purchasing and contracting team. More recently, the number of supplies divisions has been reduced to three in England, with Wales, Northern Ireland and Scotland maintaining independent supplies structures. In 1997 it is the objective of the NHSSA to produce a national catalogue of approved products, backed up by a national pricing structure. The national pricing structure will result in a dressing having a 'national contract price' for delivery from stock from a NHSSA distribution centre, although this is not the price the consumer will necessarily pay for the dressing.

These centres then add an 'on cost ' to the price of the dressing to cover their own overhead and distribution costs. This is the price that the hospitals are then charged for the dressing product. Not all dressings with a national contract price will be available from stock; to obtain a dressing that is not available from stock, a non-stock requisition would need to be raised, which would be processed through the NHSSA. The hospital can buy dressings directly from a company, but usually at a price that is higher than the national contract price. Classification of dressings varies between hospitals; in some centres, certain dressings may only be available via the hospital pharmacy.[1]

The selection and price of dressings available to community nurses is controlled by the *Drug Tariff*. This is a catalogue of items for which community pharmacists can be reimbursed by the Department of Health, when they issue a dressing against a GP's prescription. The pharmacist usually obtains the dressing from a wholesaler, who purchases the dressing directly from a company at trade price. This price consists of the *Drug Tariff* price minus wholesaler discount which the wholesaler negotiates directly from the company.

The *Drug Tariff* price in many cases is higher than the national contract price.

1.   Lewis ND (1996) personal communication

6
Modern wound dressing products are a common source of allergens

If a tissue viability nurse had a pound for every time she was told that a patient was allergic to a dressing, she would be a wealthy person.

The science behind modern wound dressings is very advanced. The companies have a lot to lose if a patient develops an allergic response to their dressing.

If a patient develops an allergic reaction to a wound dressing it is usually either a type I anaphylaxis reaction or a type IV cell-mediated reaction. A type I reaction occurs within a few minutes of the patient being exposed to the product (allergen) that they have been previously sensitised to. The effect, in the case of wound dressings, is usually localised to the dressing site. The body produces antibodies, mainly of the IgE type, which react with mast cells and basophils to produce the allergic reaction which is inflammatory in nature.[1] A type IV cell-mediated response is a delayed allergic reaction caused by activated T cells, not antibodies. The response is usually localised to the dressing site and can present as a skin eruption.[2] This explains why some patients react immediately to a dressing, whereas others do not react until the second or third application of the product.

If the product has a cream or ointment base, the carrier or preservative may be the cause of the reaction. In a study of 52 leg ulcer patients, many were found to react to the constituents of paste bandages.[3] Leg ulcer patients appear to be hypersensitive to dressing products, probably as a consequence of the battery of different products to which their ulcer has been subjected over the years. In the case of self-sealing dressings, the adhesive may cause a reaction. Sometimes, when a dressing is removed a red imprint is left behind. This is not always a reaction to the dressing, but to the wound exudate which has been allowed to pool under the dressing and macerate the skin. All of these reactions were caused by choosing inappropriate dressings which were unable to absorb the exudate.

Specific dressing products are known to stimulate allergic reactions, eg. topical antibiotics and iodine preparations. A full patient history should attempt to detect any previous allergies experienced by the patient. If the nurse is unsure whether a reaction has been caused by the dressing, he/she should perform a simple test. Apply the dressing to an area of good skin, eg. the forearm. Check the site after 12, 24, 48 and 72 hours to see if a response has occured. In the case of modern wound dressings, there is usually no reaction and incorrect dressing choice is the problem. To inform a patient that he/she is allergic to a dressing when it is not proven could deny the patient access to a valuable wound-healing resource.

If the patient is genuinely reacting to a product then a dermatologist should be consulted to deal with the problem by initiating patch testing to obtain a more accurate diagnosis.

1.   Tortora GJ, Anagnostakos NP (1990) *Principles of Anatomy and Physiology*. 6th edn. Harper Collins, New York
2.   Guyton AC, Hall JE (1996) *Textbook of Medical Physiology*. 9th edn. WB Saunders, Philadelphia
3.   Wilson CL, Cameron J, Powell SM, Cherry G, Ryan TJ (1991) High incidence of contact dermatitis in leg-ulcer patients — implications for management. *Clin Exp Dermatol* **16**: 250–3

7
An expensive dressing is a sign of quality and its ability to heal wounds quickly

Within contemporary health care the financial burden of healing cannot be ignored. Accountants are viewed as a key part of the health care team. The power has moved from the professional to the purse. As a result, cost has become part of the health equation. The cost of wound healing often focuses purely on the cost of the dressing. When assessing the cost of wound healing, two facets need to be considered: product cost and personal cost.

Product cost

This comprises individual dressing cost and total treatment cost. The total treatment cost involves:
- wound-cleansing solution, dressing pack, supplementary items, eg. swabs, secondary dressings, tape and bandages
- frequency of dressing changes
- nurse's time to cleanse and redress the wound
- associated pharmacological items, eg. vitamins
- support surfaces, ie. beds and cushions
- nurse's time to reposition the patient

Personal cost

This comprises:
- patient satisfaction
- decrease in wound pain, odour and exudate levels
- increase in self-esteem

- reduction in dependence upon health care professionals
- reduced frequency of dressing changes
- increased social contact

In order for the patient to obtain good value from a dressing, the product needs to be in place for its optimum duration. The removal of dressings for regular wound inspection defeats any attempt at obtaining optimum wear time from a dressing. The unit cost of the dressing has to be divided by its life span to get an accurate estimate of its true cost. Conventional dressings often appear cheaper per unit cost, but the need for frequent reapplications and an extended healing time result in the total treatment cost being far higher than that of a modern wound management product with a higher unit cost.

A dressing with a very high unit cost may be necessary in certain situations, eg. if there are no cheaper alternatives. A second issue is personal cost. It is vital that the patient's needs are not ignored or cast aside because of financial constraints. The nurse has a duty to provide the patient with the dressing most suitable for his/her needs and to heal his/her wounds as quickly as possible.

The wound care companies are in a very competitive market, and will have to produce evidence to show that their products are not only effective but also provide value for money.

8
A dressing has to be prescribed by a doctor before it can be used on a patient

In certain clinical areas there has been a development in the prescribing of wound dressings. Previously, only doctors could prescribe dressings for patients. The increase in nurses' knowledge of wound healing and how to optimise the process by the use of appropriate wound dressings have led to an alteration in this position. If it is thought to be beneficial to patient care, the doctor can delegate the prescribing of wound dressings to other health care personnel. Tissue viability nurses have started to prescribe wound dressings. In this situation, the medical practitioner gives written authorisation to a named person to requisition the supply and administration of a wound dressing on his/her behalf.

In order to ensure patient safety, this change in practice should be part of a prescribing policy which clearly outlines the responsibilities of all parties.

In line with the advent of nurse prescribing, the nurse should be adequately prepared for the responsibility. The process should be audited to monitor the prescribing practice of the individual.

9
Pain is sometimes inevitable during dressing changes

The control of pain in wound management has been very much underestimated.[1]

With modern wound dressings and increased knowledge, it is unacceptable for patients to suffer pain, other than minimal discomfort from dressings and the wound-dressing procedure.[2]

Hollinsworth[3] examined the methods used by nurses to assess, manage and document pain at wound-dressing changes. She concluded that teaching strategies should be developed so that nurses have a more sensitive approach which would include patient involvement in pain assessment during dressing changes, documented pain assessment and wider availability of entonox. For many years it has been known that gauze and ribbon gauze dressings can be uncomfortable *in situ* and excruciatingly painful to remove[4], and can also damage healthy granulation and epithelial tissue. Many health care professionals still choose to use these conventional dressings, however, despite the increasing use of modern dressings.

Many dressings are known to be almost painless to remove; they include hydrogels, hydrocolloids, non-adherent membranes[5], alginates and hydrocellular foams.[6]

1. Thomas S (1989) Pain and wound management. *Community Outlook* **July**: 11–15
2. Williams C (1996) Painful dressings. *J Tiss Viability* **6**(3): 69–70
3. Hollinsworth H (1995) Nurses' assessment and management of pain at wound dressing changes. *J Wound Care* **4**(2): 77–83
4. Gibson C (1993) Cavity dressings ancient and modern: a little research. *Br J Theatre Nurs* **3**(1): 8–10
5. Williams C (1995) Mepitel. *Br J Nurs* **4**(1): 51–5
6. Williams C (1995) Allevyn. *Br J Nurs* **4**(2): 107–10

10
Hydrogels are only suitable for the treatment of sloughy and necrotic wounds

Hydrogels can be used during all stages of the wound-healing process[1]. Recently, the use of hydrogels in other areas of skin and wound care has been reported.[2] Other areas of use include:

- The management of cavity wounds, in combination with a non-woven gauze. Adherence to delicate granulation tissue is rare as the hydrogel promotes a moist environment

- Dermatological skin conditions such as dermatitis artefact, flexural psoriasis and pemphigus foliaceus

- Inflamed skin flexures occurring in natural folds, eg. under breasts and in the groin and abdomen. Hydrogels can be applied to the affected areas with a low adherent dressing to separate the skin folds

- Radiotherapy can damage the skin causing erythema, dry desquamation or moist desquamation. Hydrogels have been used in all three conditions, and can be used while the patient is receiving radiotherapy

- Hydrogels have been used for many years in the management of extravasation injuries in neonates, in the form of a hydrogel boot or glove

- Excoriation of the skin is a common problem in incontinent patients. A hydrogel can be applied like a cream to the affected area, following cleansing after each bout of incontinence

- Hydrogels have also been used in the management of fistula and nappy rash

Much of the evidence is anecdotal, but there does seem to be a place for extension of the role of hydrogels.

1. Thomas S (1994) Wound cleansing agents. *J Wound Care* **3**(7): 325–8
2. Williams C (1995) Intrasite Gel: the extended role. Poster presentation. *Proceedings of 5th European Conference on Advances in Wound Management, 21–24 November, Harrogate.* Macmillan Magazines, London: 285

11
Adhesive dressings should not be used on excoriated skin

It is possible to use adhesive dressings[1,2,3] and semi-permeable films[4] on excoriated skin.

The nurse must first undertake a holistic assessment to determine the underlying cause. Excoriation may be due to incontinence, drainage from a fistula[5], perspiration or wound exudate.

Protective skin wipes can be used on intact skin. The wipes that are currently available come in the form of a small pad. The sealant dries to form a thin film over the skin.[6]

Adhesive dressings, semi-permeable films and tapes therefore adhere to the thin film and not to the skin. Dealey[7] found that this type of treatment regimen was effective in reducing erythema.

Cavilon, no string barrier film (a 'wand' application system rather than a small square pad), is available in Europe but not in the UK at the moment. It will be available shortly. Cavilon is siloxane based rather than alcohol based and is said to be easier to apply and to cause less pain or stinging than alcohol-based products.[8] It was reported to be equally effective in protecting the skin.

1. Williams C (1994) Spyrosorb and Spyroflex. *Br J Nurs* **3**(12): 628–30
2. Williams C (1994) Tielle: a hydropolymer dressing *Br J Nurs* **3**(19): 1029–30
3. Williams C, Young T (1996) Allevyn adhesive. *Br J Nurs* **5**(11): 691–3
4. Williams C (1995) Opsite Flexigrid. *Br J Nurs* **4**(7): 411–14
5. Phillips J, Walton M (1992) Caring for patients with enterocutaneous fistula. *Br J Nurs* **1**(10): 496–500
6. Dealey C (1995) Common problems in wound care: caring for the skin around wounds. *Br J Nurs* **4**(1): 43–4

7. Dealey C (1992) Using protective skin wipes under adhesive tapes. *J Wound Care* **1**(2): 19–22
8. Rolstad BS, Borchert K, Magnan S, Scheel N (1994) A comparison of an alcohol-based and a siloxane-based per-wound skin protectant. *J Wound Care* **3**(8): 367–8

12
The best dressing for a graft and donor site is paraffin gauze

Paraffin gauze has traditionally been used as a primary wound contact layer for grafts and donor sites for many years, but this does not make it the best dressing. There are several problems/disadvantages associated with such a dressing:

1. Paraffin gauze is known to adhere to the wound. Removal of the dressing causes extra pain, can damage newly formed epithelial and granulation tissue, and can dislodge grafts, all of which will delay wound healing. Granulation tissue can also grow through the mesh of the dressing and be pulled off during removal.

2. Because the constituents of the dressing are water-repellent, removal of the dressing is not facilitated by soaking in warm saline.

The principles of moist wound healing should be used at all times. Modern wound dressings, such as non-adherent membranes, hydrocolloids and alginates, provide an excellent environment for wound healing and have all been used successfully in the management of grafts and donor sites. There is now no place for the traditional and often painful alternatives.[1]

1.Young T (1995) Burns and scalds. *Practice Nurse* **6**(18): 37–40

No 13
Silver nitrate is the treatment of choice for overgranulating wounds

Before commencing treatment of overgranulation, the nurse must undertake a full holistic assessment to confirm the diagnosis as carcinoma can also present as a sudden exuberant growth of tissue in a chronic non-healing wound.[1]

Many treatment options have been described in the literature. They include:

Silver nitrate — this is a traditional treatment, but has many disadvantages. It has been described as a caustic form of treatment and prolonged use may cause many problems, eg. hypocalcaemia, hyponatraemia and a black staining which could hinder wound assessment.

Topical corticosteroids — preparations of these agents may contain potential allergens, causing further skin problems, and it is recommended that they only are used under medical supervision. Application to the wound bed may retard wound closure.

Surgical excision — this would re-initiate the inflammatory phase of wound healing and may perpetuate the cycle of events.

Non-traumatic treatments are a much more viable option. They include the use of a polyurethane foam, a temporary change of primary dressing from occlusive to non-occlusive, application of light pressure, or taking no action at all, as in many cases the overgranulation will resolve spontaneously.

1.   Young T (1995) Common problems in wound care: overgranulation. *Br J Nurs* **4**(3): 169–70

14
Alginates should be moistened before application

Alginate dressings are versatile materials which can be used in the management of most types of exuding wounds. They are of little value if applied to a dry or lightly exuding wound.[1]

Alginate dressings vary in absorbency, but typically will absorb 15–20 times their own weight of exudate[1].

Some alginates are high in mannuronic acid and produce a soft gel,[2] whereas others are high in guluronic acid and produce a firmer gel.[3]

Alginates have been designed specifically for highly exuding wounds; moistening them would therefore reduce their ability to absorb exudate and encourage their use in an area for which they were not intended.

1.   Thomas S (1992) Alginates. *J Wound Care* **1**(1): 29–32
2.   Williams C (1994) Sorbsan. *Br J Nurs* **3**(13): 677–80
3.   Williams C (1994) Kaltostat. *Br J Nurs* **3**(18): 965–7

15
Stoma products can be used for wound care

Some wounds produce such large amounts of exudate or fluid drainage that stoma products are the only viable treatment option. Some stoma-type products have been designed specifically as wound managers.[1]

The most common wound requiring a stoma product is a fistula. A fistula is an abnormal tract connecting two epithelial surfaces.[2] The most common type is an enterocutaneous fistula, which connects an internal organ and the skin.

In order to create the optimal environment for fistula closure the health care professional must pay particular attention to the care of the skin and the fistula, nutritional supplements, and control of sepsis.[3]

Careful preparation of the wound and the skin is essential if wound drainage bags are to be successful. The skin edges need to be protected by a protective skin wipe (but only on intact skin) or an extra thin hydrocolloid before application of a filler paste.[4] This is often followed by the application of a hydrocolloid wafer and then the wound drainage bag.

To ensure a successful outcome, it is essential that wound management is a multidisciplinary team effort.

Stoma products have a useful role to play in the management of these difficult wounds.

1.   McLean F, Hale C (1990) Comparing drainage bags. *Nurs Times* **86**(15): 66–9
2.   Phillips J, Walton M (1992) Caring for patients with enterocutaneous fistulae. *Br J Nurs* **1**(10): 496–500
3.   Borwell B (1994) Nursing management of the patient with a gastro-intestinal fistula. *J Tiss Viability* **4**(1): 23–6
4.   Pringle WK (1995) The management of patients with enterocutaneous fistulas. *J Wound Care* **4**(5): 211–13

16
Hydrocolloid dressings cannot be used on neonates

The skin of a premature baby born at or before 28 weeks is immature. The barrier function of the epidermis is not fully effective. It matures within two weeks of birth, the maturation being stimulated by the changes from a fluid environment in the uterus to an air environment.[1]

Premature babies are often poorly and, as a consequence, are subjected to many external procedures that result in tissue trauma. The skin is extremely delicate and the small size of the babies' limbs makes wound dressing problematic.

If the wound is not managed correctly, there is the risk of scarring and loss of function of the affected area.

Wounds often occur on the limbs, as these are the sites used for insertion of intravenous cannulae. The treatment for limb wounds is to bag the limb with a hydrogel.[2] Unfortunately, if the limb is very tiny the weight of the gel is too heavy for the baby.

Hydrocolloid dressings may at first sight appear to be excessively adhesive for the skin of a premature baby. However, in a study carried out in two special care baby units, DuoDerm extra thin hydrocolloid dressings were used successfully to heal wounds in babies born prematurely. Three types of wounds included:

- extravasation injuries
- shearing due to tape
- electrode damage

Wounds often healed within one week and the dressing also provided a barrier to infection and protection against further injury.[3]

1.   Young T (1995) Wound healing in neonates. *J Wound Care* **4**(6): 285–8

2.   Williams C (1994) Intrasite gel: a hydrogel dressing. *Br J Nurs* **3**(16): 843–6
3.   Young T, Atkinson J, Irving VE (1997) The use of a hydrocolloid dressing in the treatment of iatrogenic neonatal skin trauma. *Proceedings of Sixth European Conference on Advances in Wound Management*. Macmillan Magazines, London

17
Eusol has a role to play in wound care

Some regard the evidence against hypochlorites as strong enough to class them as a disinfectant rather than an antiseptic, and therefore unsuitable for use in the treatment of wounds.[1] However, a significant body of medical opinion still favours the use of hypochlorites for cleansing and debriding sloughy or necrotic wounds.

Nurses have been accused of effectively banning eusol without appropriate consultation and for no good reason.

Eusol has been shown to be cytotoxic, to damage granulating tissue and epithelial tissue, to prolong the inflammatory response, to cause hyperthermia and burn, localised oedema and local cell toxicity, to reduce collagen synthesis and the microcirculation, to cause irritation and pain, and to lead to acute renal failure and hypernatraemia.[2]

The eusol issue raises a number of important legal and professional issues for nurses.[3] Only the individual practitioner can take the decision to prescribe or treat a wound with a hypochlorite once all the factors relating to the patient have been weighed and assessed.[2]

The evidence suggests that hypochlorites are too risky for use in wound treatment and the practitioner should consider a safer alternative such as hydrogels, enzymes or hydrocolloids.

1. Moore DJ (1996) The use of antiseptics in wound care. Critique III. *J Wound Care* **5**(1): 44–7
2. Moore DJ (1992) Hypochlorites: a review of the evidence. *J Wound Care* **1**(4): 44–53
3. Tingle J (1990) Eusol and the law. *Nurs Times* **86**(38): 70–2

18
Hydrocolloid dressings cause overgranulation

Overgranulation is the presence of a raised red gelatinous mass that protrudes above the level of the surrounding skin. It is also known as hypergranulation, proud flesh, hypertrophic granulation and hyperplasia of granulation tissue. The cause is unknown, but is linked to a prolonged inflammatory phase of wound healing, although overgranulation does not present until the third proliferative phase of wound healing.

Overgranulation can occur in all types of wounds. It prevents final healing being achieved, as the epithelial cells do not migrate over the overgranulation tissue as they would do over normal granulation tissue in the fourth phase of wound healing.

Anecdotally the formation of overgranulation has been linked to hydrocolloid dressings. There are two reasons for this supposition:

1. Hydrocolloids are frequently used during the third phase of wound healing when the overgranulation is visible.[1]

2. Hydrocolloids promote the formation of granulation tissue. This is one of their attributes and the reason for choosing them as a dressing option.[2]

However, to date there is no proof that hydrocolloids cause overgranulation. Personal experience also challenges the myth. Patients who develop overgranulation while receiving treatment with hydrocolloid dressings have carried on with the dressing and the overgranulation has resolved and the wound healed. Consequently, the statement that hydrocolloid dressings cause overgranulation is, at present, an unsubstantiated myth.

1. Young T (1995) Common problems in wound care: overgranulation. *Pract Nurse* **6**(11): 14,16
2. Young T (1997) Use of a hydrocolloid in overgranulation. *J Wound Care* **6**(5): 216

19
Surgical wounds require daily dressing changes

The frequency of dressing changes depends on the condition of the wound bed, not on the time of day.

Surgical wounds heal by primary intention following closure of the skin and underlying tissue with either sutures or staples. Closure of the wound provides the body with the optimum type of defence — its own skin. The void beneath the sutures will heal by the formation of granulating tissue and epithelial cell migration. The amount of tissue loss is smaller than in open wounds that are left to heal by secondary intention, therefore the void will be filled rapidly.[1] Provided that the wound edges are together and the wound appears visually closed, the wound does not require a dressing to facilitate healing and can be safely left exposed.[2]

Postoperative dressings have often consisted of a dry pad (eg. gauze) with an adhesive edge. These do not allow examination of the wound. They absorb immediate postoperative exudate, dry out and then adhere to the wound, thus causing pain on removal.[3] The nurse should question the purpose of this postoperative dressing. Often it is seen as a method of protecting the wound against external friction, such as that caused by bed clothes and nightwear. If so, then daily changes will cause rather than prevent trauma. It is not waterproof and prevents the patient from bathing/showering in the postoperative period.

If protection is required then a vapour-permeable film dressing is an ideal solution. It can contain a minimal amount of exudate, is transparent to allow wound inspection, waterproof to allow bathing and only requires changing on a weekly basis. The moist environment keeps sutures moist and prevents crusting, which can be a problem on dressing removal. This type of dressing also acts as a barrier to bacteria and reduces the risk of cross-infection.[4]

If the wound has become clinically infected, it will require dressing on a daily basis to remove the copious amount of exudate and debris produced by such a wound. In this situation the suture line will usually have broken down. As the wound heals, the dressing regimen can be modified, reverting to weekly dressings and minimal intervention as soon as possible.

1.   Chrintz H, Vibits H, Codtz TO, Hareby JS, Waaddeg-Gard P, Larsen SO (1989) Need for surgical wound dressings. *Br J Surgery* **76**(2): 204–5
2.   Gilchrist B (1990) Washing and dressings after surgery. *Nurs Times* **86**(50): 71
3.   Hulten L (1994) Dressings for surgical wounds. *Am J Surg* **167**(1A Suppl): 42s–45s
4.   Young T (1996) Methicillin-resistant *Staphylococcus aureus*. *J Wound Care* **5**(10): 475–7

20
All wound dressings should be sterile

When dressing a wound, it is essential that the dressing is sterile. Even though the wound bed itself may not be sterile, the dressing has to be sterile. The potential for the introduction of contamination into the wound bed exists if the dressing is not sterile. Wound contamination would be extremely problematic for an immunocompromised patient. Dressings stored in a hospital environment are potentially susceptible to contamination by airborne pathogens.

Wound-dressing products are usually sterilised by gamma radiation. The method of sterilisation and the expiry date are specified on the packaging.

In-house items such as wound dressing packs and packets of theatre swabs are autoclaved and sterilised by steam. These will also have a date stamp but this may be the date of sterilisation. The Bow Dick check (the stripes on the tape) is confirmation of the sterilisation process.

The use of dressings from an opened pack, even if used for one patient only, is suspect practice. It could delay rather than accelerate the wound-healing process, and increase the personal and financial cost of wound healing. This is often done in an attempt to save wastage, but is usually contrary to the manufacturers' instructions.

Conclusion

Wound care is often described as the bread and butter of nursing. It is an essential procedure in many areas of nursing, each area having its own needs and complications.

This book has attempted to demystify many of the myths surrounding wound care.

At times it appears that wound care is scientifically advancing at great speed, with, for example, the advent of tissue engineering and research into scarless wound healing. The practical application of the theory still complies with the obligatory time lag, taking 30 years for moist wound healing to become accepted into clinical practice. The time lag, although inevitable, should not be compulsory. Many forward-thinking practitioners are, through reflective practice, already questioning their standard of wound care delivery.

This book has, hopefully, provided an indication of sound wound care practice and identified many of the dubious practices that are still accepted as the 'norm' in some clinical areas.

The themes of holistic assessment and a multidisciplinary approach have pervaded the text and identified the path forward. Too often, individual disciplines attempt to grasp and own wound care, territorialising its ownership. This will not produce the best outcome for the patient. Mutual recognition of the role of the multidisciplinary team is nowhere more evident than in wound care. The surgeon can debride and often revascularise ischaemic tissue; the physician can improve oxygen delivery to the tissues; the dietician can provide the vital ingredients with which to repair tissue; and the physiotherapist can assist in returning the patient to a state of optimum mobility. Nurses can assess, dress and nurture the patient and his/her wound. They can coordinate the input of the team and lead the team towards goals that are identified in conjunction with the patient and carer.

In order to facilitate the optimum wound care for the patient, the nurse must ensure that her knowledge base is sound and that the care delivered is, where possible, research-based. It may be enlightening for readers to reattempt the myth/reality quiz at the end of the book to see whether their knowledge base has improved.

This book is the first step in improving the wound care delivered by nurses to patients. It will hopefully eliminate the archaic practices that exist and prevent current practitioners from becoming the dinosaurs who still advocate many of the myths dispelled by this book.

SELF-ASSESSMENT QUESTIONNAIRE

The aim of this questionnaire is for you to identify deficits in your knowledge of wound care.

After reading the book you will, hopefully, have expanded your knowledge; by repeating the questionnaire you can evaluate whether learning has taken place.

Question one

List the four stages of wound healing

1

2

3

4

Question two

List five factors that delay wound healing

1

2

3

4

5

Question three

List two benefits of wound exudate

1

2

Question four

List three characteristics of an ideal wound environ- ment

1

2

3

Question five

List two local and two systemic signs of wound infection

local

1

2

systemic

1

2

Question six

List three methods of wound cleansing

1

2

3

Question seven

How do you treat a wound infection?

Topical antibiotics ❏

Systemic antibiotics ❏

A combination of the two ❏

Question eight

List three mechanical causes of pressure sores

1

2

3

Question nine

List three pressure sore risk assessment scales

1

2

3

Question ten

How long does it take for a pressure sore to develop

1 hour ❑

2 hours ❑

6 hours ❑

12 hours ❑

24 hours ❑

48 hours ❑

1 week ❑

Question eleven

List six types of leg ulcers

1

2

3

4

5

6

Question twelve

Below which of the following ABPI readings is it unsafe to apply compression bandaging?

1.5 ❏

1.0 ❏

0.8 ❏

0.5 ❏

Question thirteen

List three compression bandaging regimens

1

2

3

Question fourteen

How often should a dressing be changed?

every day ❏

every two days ❏

every five days ❏

every week ❏

other ▭

Index

B

Barrier cream improves the quality of the skin to such a degree that it is less likely to develop into a pressure sore 89

Bathing with an open wound is an unsafe practice   56

Both very thin people and very fat people are at risk of developing pressure sores   83

C

Cardiac and respiratory disease do not have an adverse effect on wound healing   20

Circular and figure-of-eight bandaging techniques result in different levels of compression   117

D

Debridement is a method of wound cleansing   60

Diabetic ulcers are caused by peripheral vascular disease 124

District nurses do not have access to the same range of dressings as hospital nurses 135

Dressings can be used in combination to make a more efficient product   133

E

Erythema around the wound edges is confirmation of wound infection   47

Eusol has a role to play in wound care   156

G

Gloves should be used for all dressings   75

H

Haematological investigations are an important part of the wound assessment process   13

Healing is complete when epithelial tissue covers the wound   4

Hospital and community staff pay the same price for their dressing products   138

Human immuno deficiency virus (HIV) cannot be contracted via wound exudate   73

Hydrocolloid dressings cannot be used on neonates   154

Hydrocolloid dressings cause overgranulation   157

Hydrogels are only suitable for the treatment of sloughy and necrotic wounds   146

Hydrogen peroxide can help to clean traumatic wounds   58

Hyperbaric oxygen is a proven aid to wound healing   35

Hypertrophic and keloid are two ways of describing abnormal scarring   30

I

If a dressing has not worked in three days then it needs to be changed to another product 132

If a leg ulcer has a mixed aetiology it is not possible to use compression therapy   121

It is not possible to have a pressure sore in a neonate   84

It is not possible to identify erythema in a coloured person 85

It is possible, through good nursing care, to prevent all pressure sores 78

K
Keeping a wound warm will increase the number of bacteria and delay healing 43

L
Leeches have a place in modern wound management 33

Leg ulcer is a diagnosis 104

M
Maggots have a place in modern wound management 32

Measuring interface pressure is the only way of evaluating the effectiveness of a support surface 100

Men and women are equally likely to suffer from a leg ulcer 106

Methylated spirit/spirit pads can be a useful preventive measure in pressure sore development 88

Modern wound dressing products are a common source of allergens 140

N
Nutritional supplements will only aid healing if the patient is underweight 26

O
Only patients using wheelchairs require a pressure-relieving cushion 94

Only venous leg ulcers occur in the gaiter area 112

P
Pain is sometimes inevitable during dressing changes 145

Patients with leg ulcers should not have a shower or bath in case their ulcer gets wet 107

Patients with methicillin-resistant *Staphyloccocus aureus* (MRSA) in their wounds should be nursed in an isolation cubicle 71

Poor surgical technique is the most common cause of wound breakdown 67

Pressure sores are not only caused by pressure shearing forces and friction are also important factors 80

Pressure sores are the responsibility of the multidisciplinary team and not just the nurse 79

R
Research has shown that massaging and rubbing pressure areas increases the circulation and reduces the risk of pressure sore development 86

Research has proved that sitting a patient on a rubber or air-filled ring can cause more damage and does not help to prevent pressure sores 95